CARRY ON

Stan Zuray's Journey
from Boston Greaser
to Alaskan Homesteader

Stan Zuray
&
Tim Attewell

Dedicated to my Mom and Dad.
Love, Stanley

CONTENTS

Preface From Tim Attewell

In his youth, Stan did questionable things. As a homesteader, he did difficult ones. He relishes none of these acts, and this book is not intended to encourage them.

The names of some people have been altered to protect their identities.

The role of Charlotte, Stan's first wife and homesteading partner, has been reduced out of respect for her privacy.

This is not intended to be a guidebook for anyone looking to run away from society and into the wilderness. Stan views himself as a survivor of his own life. Times have changed. Hitchhiking, open federal land, and the days of being invited into a stranger's home have long since gone. For these reasons, Stan may have been one of the last to walk this wild path...

...which makes his story incredibly important to tell

Stan

On the Natural Life

There's this romanticized vision of leaving civilization to live among the trees. Being "one with nature," is an ideal that a lot of people seem to fantasize over, but being one with anything means being one with all of it, not just a few selected parts. Beauty is only half of nature. There is a brutal side as well.

I don't claim to have really been "one with nature," though, and I don't want to talk up the brutality. I do want to dispel a myth: There was very little romance to the lifestyle, because there was so little time to think, and actually enjoy it. I was in a constant state of motion. Each season meant preparing for the next.

I'm not complaining, though. It was the kind of work I wanted to do.

Chapter 1
Fire

Alaskan Interior. June 1, 1973.

It sounded like a jet engine and looked like daylight, though the sun had not yet risen and no airliners would ever make a low pass over this patch of the Alaskan wilderness. Stan awoke not just to the sound and light, but incredible heat. He scrambled out of his tent to see a crackling, roaring inferno consuming everything he owned. The flames climbed high above the shack and onto the four enormous, seventy-foot spruce trees it had been constructed around. The result was an eighty-foot tower of fire in the middle of the Tozitna River Valley, forty miles from the nearest village.

"The dogs!" Charlotte's voice broke Stan's trance and the young couple immediately split up. Charlotte rushed to put out the various brush fires that had sprung up all around them. Stan raced to rescue the five sled dogs that were chained up dangerously close to the fire.

He got to Skipper first, a loyal half-wolf, half Newfoundland Labrador that had been with him since the beginning of his journey into Alaska. Skipper had the keenest senses of all five of the dogs, and would often pick up the scent of an approaching bear fifteen minutes before the rest of the team. Now he was barking up a storm at the hot nightmare that had invaded his territory.

"Down! Easy!" Stan did his best to hold the dog still between his knees. Skipper's whiskers had long since melted down to the fur. Every part of Stan that faced the fire was hit by terrible heat. The stinging sensation all over his body served to remind him; he was doing all of this wearing only his underwear.

Well this is going well, Stan thought, fumbling for the chain's release. *One month in the wilderness and we've just lost our food, clothing, shelter, tools, guns, gunpowder*—BANG—*and our ammo.*

What had previously been their cook shack and living area was now transformed into a bag of hostile popcorn. Once the first round exploded, Stan knew one hundred and fifty more would follow. There was a suitcase, absolutely packed full of ammo, right at the fire's center. Stan released Skipper, who immediately ran to a safe distance and established a defensive barking perimeter around the invasive hot monster.

On to the next dog. Stan held an arm high to shield his eyes from any stray bullets. He wasn't overly concerned about the rifle rounds, though. Without the containment of a chamber and gun barrel, the bullets were dangerous, but not fatal. In most cases, once the powder blew the bullet wouldn't travel far. Instead, the momentum would be applied to the much lighter shell casing, which would spin off wildly.

This was a lesson Stan learned during childhood days in Boston, while making zip guns in his parent's basement. He and his rascal friends would often snap the antennas from cars, use them as gun barrels, and test fire the one-shot weapons beneath a stack of newspapers to muffle the sound. If a zip gun survived the test, they would take it out at night and unleash hellish lead on the neighborhood streetlights. Now Stan felt impossibly far from those Boston nights.

He pushed the exploding, loose rounds from his mind, and focused on the real danger. His twelve-gauge shotgun was somewhere in the flames, and it was loaded. In hindsight, leaving a shell in the barrel seemed like a mistake; but how was he to know he would be starting a forest fire tonight?

In his mind, Stan could see the loaded gun standing there amidst the flames. It had likely already fallen from its place, and once the heat reached the right intensity, it would let loose. Which direction would the blast fly? It could be any one out of the three hundred and sixty degrees that circled the tent. Stan figured he had at least those odds of taking a round of buckshot somewhere on his body before he got the dogs free.

Cleetsa was next. A tiny, cream-colored dog, she was leader of Stan's team. Her bark was more of a yelp compared to Skipper's, and Stan got an earful of it. The giant popcorn bag in front of him kept cooking, and Stan felt a burning sensation on his knees that was more intense than the current norm. He looked down to see that the grass all around him had caught fire. Beneath it, hot embers had already formed. He unclasped the chain and Cleetsa bolted off, just as a *one-two-three pop* of bullets fired out of the tent.

Onward he rushed, through the burn. The fire's updraft was so strong that it was pulling a breeze across Stan's skin, and into the blaze. There were three more dogs. Minto, who was acquired from the village of the same name. Next there was Monk and Rocky. Both had been given to Stan in Tanana, along with Cleetsa. He ran to each of them, repeating the same process, one after another.

Once all the dogs were loose, Stan and Charlotte could only do one thing. They ran down the riverbank for cover and watched as everything they needed to survive was reduced to ash. Their dog sled had been leaning on the shack. The snowshoes that Stan had so painstakingly handcrafted before leaving Boston had been sitting on the roof. Their food and clothing had just been eliminated from the delicate equation of homesteading.

"Are you ok?" Stan didn't realize it until he spoke, but he was panting.

"I've had better nights," claimed Charlotte, and Stan took the joke to mean she hadn't been burned any worse than he had. The adrenaline of the moment was keeping them high, but once it wore off they would return to an unkind reality.

Stan looked over past the fire, to their future cabin. It was still only a home-in-progress. Though safe from the flames, at this point it was only three logs high, and more a giant picture frame than a place of shelter for the winter. Stan got the sense that the dream was dead before it had even started. He wondered how he would complete the cabin before winter without tools or food to fuel the process. Tired of the burning imagery, Stan and Charlotte turned to lie down on the bank. Stan was twenty-three, and Charlotte twenty-one. Alone in the wilderness, they listened to the exploding rounds like thunder of an approaching storm.

Stan
On His Youth

My time in Alaska wasn't just a strange turn in life. It was a direct product of my childhood. It would be tough to understand how or why I became a homesteader without knowing about my time in Boston.

I always say that parents show you your options in life, for better or worse. As children, I think we're constantly taking down a mental list of things to do later in life. My parents raised me around gardens, clam digging, and fishing. My father taught me how to make something out of nothing, and displayed a bottomless work ethic.

I'm thankful for good parents. They cut my path out of the city. The turmoil, crime, drugs, and final loneliness made sure that I would never come back to stay.

Chapter 2
Lost

Boston. April, 1959.

From above, the blacktop crawls with motion, much like an ant mound. The pitter-patter of children's shoes on the ground forms a sort of chaotic drum beat to a song with lyrics of screams and laughter. This is recess at Thomas J. Kenny School.

Just east of the schoolyard is an empty lot, hosting a mix of dirt, grass, and weeds. A boy plays alone in this lot; or rather, he quests. He searches the vacant land high and low for signs of life. Mice and snakes are common in these parts. In the boy's peripheral vision, he sees a small shape scurrying between rocks. He crouches at first and observes the mouse for a moment. In one snapping jolt, he breaks into an all out run and—

Time runs on.

The boy's classmates have grown like rockets. They tower over him now. Being the shortest boy in middle school is a precarious place. One of the classmates smears black ink on the boy's expensive church suit; his mother won't be able to salvage it. The next day, the boy is kicked off of his bike, and into his first fight. He does not fare well.

The fire station smells of oil. Sparks rain down onto damp cement as the boy's father, a welder, finishes another contract for the fire department. It's after school, and the boy's father tells him that he can fix anything in the world. It is a lesson that will carry the boy far one day. Standing between him and that journey are many things, time being one of them. It—

Moves on.

He plays in the wet sand while his father goes clam digging on the beach. High castles and deep trenches occupy the boy's mind. His father wears a pair of rubber waders out into the waves. The waders will one day be passed down, and keep the boy dry as he crosses an Alaskan river to harvest the meat from his first grizzly bear kill. Like that river's current, time—

Flows on.

Finally, he understands the hype. The boy steps out of the theater, wide-eyed. *West Side Story* has all of the neighborhood kids excited about street life and gangs. The boy is pulled into an alley right next to the theater, pinned to the wall, and held at knifepoint by the same bully that started the boy's fighting career. The blade is only one inch long, not made to kill but to teach a lesson. The boy mouths off to the bully in defiance. The knife goes in. The boy, now eleven years old, clutches his bleeding gut as he walks home.

At his first job, the boy learns a great deal. He sees his boss stealing from the manager, he sees the manager stealing from the owner, and he gets an idea or two of how the world works. He also learns the value of certain hubcaps and how easily they can be removed.

By less than honest means, the boy acquires his first pair of wire-wheel hubcaps. He sells them to his math teacher and, lo and behold, he receives straight As in trigonometry for the rest of the year.

A group of older kids takes notice of the boy and his skills. He's younger and shorter, but he's crazy, and the other kids like that. He teaches them the trade of theft, and in return is accepted as one of them. The leader of the pack calls the boy "Stumples," but for the first time in the boy's life, it's a friendly nickname. He starts to work out; he's getting stronger now. With his new friends, he isn't picked on so much anymore. As he pumps the weights, time—

Presses on.

There's trouble on the block. The boy doesn't understand exactly what kind. He never does. He's too young to hear the intricate workings of the gang. Still, he gives his weapon of choice—a two foot long chain—a few practice twirls and all at once, the enemy appears.

The rival gang stands ominously at the other end of the block. Another kid, slightly older, lets out a war cry, and everything is set in motion. The rumble is on. With fifteen allies at his side, the boy charges into combat, ready to swing his chain at the first person he meets. Fathers are at work. Mothers are screaming.

The battle concludes, and the boy's name is defended by his fiery Irish mother. She shouts that her son would never fight, but inside she knows exactly what he's done. The boy is sent to his room.

Time rolls on.

The hubcaps are selling, and the parking lots of grocery stores make perfect hunting grounds for the boy and his friends. Until the day the police catch them red handed. The boy is taken home to his mother. He's only thirteen, and he has been in trouble with the police countless times already. His parents are approaching their wits' end. No amount of trouble is enough to deter the boy from his chosen lifestyle.

"If this is what you're going to do with your life," says the boy's father, "don't be stupid about it. You're going to end up in jail for something like hubcaps. Be smart. Plan it out. Rob a bank. Do it right and make a lot of money. Do something creative and get away with it."

The boy doesn't think his father is serious about the bank, but he recognizes something worse than anger or disappointment. The boy's father seems ready to give up on him. Time, on the other hand—

Rolls on.

The boy has amassed nearly one hundred General Motors car keys from friends working at junk yards by now. One by one, he sifts through a ring of his twenty most reliable keys, trying them in the car's ignition at his favorite hunting ground. His older friends watch eagerly, ready to bolt if they must. A man steps out of the grocery and walks towards his car. The man's car fires up without him, and the boy drives away with his first score.

Alcoholic Beverage Commission IDs enter the scene. One of the boy's friends steals ten, and now they can get into any club or bar of their choosing. The "combat zone" in Boston is a place of strip bars, vice cops, prostitutes, and above all: music.

The boy watches, mesmerized, as the soul musicians roll up in their black Cadillacs, and step out like giants. He stands at the back of the bar enjoying the powerful talent of Sam and Dave performing

"Hold on, I'm Comin'." The boy's hair is slicked back. He wears a leather jacket. He's a greaser now. He and his friends make good money selling fake IDs to other youngsters in Boston. He's fifteen years old, and feels as though he could be king.

Time slides on.

His parents scrounge up the money they need. The boy's father is up for promotion, but he won't get it if he doesn't pay the boss. Three-hundred dollars means a lot to them, but it's a wise investment, and this is the way things are. The next day, the boy sees his father walk into the fire chief's office with an envelope. It seems that corruption isn't restricted to the body shop; it's the way of the world, and the world—

Spins on.

The hotrod screams like a missile launch. It better; the boy has put his heart and soul into the thing. He's even paid for some of the parts. Light as a feather, with the torque of a small moon, the boy takes the race. He laughs as he and his homemade machine cross the finish line.

Across an ocean, a conflict between capitalism and communism reaches its boiling point. The draft is called, and many of the boy's older friends are shipped off to Vietnam. He is, yet again, left to his own devices.

Time marches on.

The boy works all summer long to pay for college. He knows he can't be a screw up for the rest of his life. It's time to get an education and some kind of job, maybe in insurance. He's not just a boy anymore, but he still has his wild heart. He picks fights; wins some and loses others. Outside of a bar, he's stabbed for the second time in his life. This knife is bigger, and the wound in his chest is slow to heal.

The boy's friends begin returning from overseas, a few bring something with them. Heroin decimates what social scene the boy had left. Loyalty and sanity seem to vanish overnight. The boy avoids heroin, but not by moral high ground or smart thinking. He simply hates needles. Now he sits in a bar with the man that once protected him and called him "Stumples." The man cries about the things that he saw in Vietnam. They're unspeakable. The boy sips his beer, wondering when his own draft notice will come.

Time drips on.

The boy has grown so accustomed to psychedelic drugs that he can speak to cops while high on LSD. Working alone tonight, he steals a car. He's lost track of how many there were before this. It's December and the Boston cold is unforgiving. The boy rolls one block before lights and sirens start up behind him. He floors it. Looking back at the police, the boy catches a glimpse of something. Behind him, there is a child's car seat, and a stack of Christmas presents.

What am I doing?

He races down streets and alleys, turning erratically, hoping to evade the cop. He hops the curb, careens across the grass of a neighborhood park and vanishes around a corner. The boy walks away from the car, leaving his ring of keys on the seat. He has finally stolen his last car.

Time seems to pivot that night, then rolls on.

The boy hears of a mansion up north. It was once the home of a rock band called Far Cry. Now it is a commune, and a place of learning. He visits the mansion for a weekend and proves his worth. *You can fix anything,* his father once said, and that included the mansion's boiler. The boy returns to Boston long enough to drop out of college, and moves north, into the commune. For a while, he keeps the place running. He lives in a Visqueen shack in the woods behind the mansion. For warmth in the winter, the boy maintains his first wood-burning stove. Life here lasts him a while, but time—

Interferes

The boy receives his draft notice, but that's a story for another—

Time.

A man from a catholic monastery visits the commune. He teaches the boy about spirituality, meditation and yoga. It is the first time the boy hears the term "high on life," and he starts to move away from drugs.

The boy's hotrod is nearing its final miles. He pulls into a gas station and trades it in for a Volkswagen.

Now he meditates. He dreams he's stuck in a well. Hands and feet pressing against the walls, holding him up. Above him, looking down, are smiling faces, but these are no friendly smiles. He struggles to climb out, but each time he takes his hand off the wall, he slips further down. The smiling faces refuse to help. He wakes up from the dream and for days his life seems off kilter.

The boy is anxious and unsettled until he meditates again. The dream of the well returns to him. He sees the faces above him again. They are the society he's struggling to live within. He questions if making it out of the hole will truly bring him happiness, and in that moment, he lets go. The boy falls, into blackness at first, and then: a wide-open, grassy field. There's not a single person in sight. The boy wakes up, feeling for once that everything will be ok.

The locals don't approve of hippies, though. Many try to have the commune shut down. It becomes clear to the boy that this is a place without a future. Reluctantly, he, with time—

Moves on.

The boy lives on a boat in dry dock. He dreams of one day taking it south along the coast to find a tropical island, but that day never comes; he is destined for colder places. He picks up work on a fishing boat and begins learning the trade. Years from now, fishing a different kind of fish in a different kind of water will keep the boy from going hungry, but first—

Time.

"You're gonna get off that boat," says a police officer. "Or we're going to find some dope on you." Hippies are not welcome in the harbor either. The boy sells the boat. He leaves, but this time he'll go much further.

Time.

He pours himself over a map, looking for solitude. He craves a quiet corner of the continent away from the hustle and corruption of city living.

Time.

He packs some clothes into his VW Beetle, finally ready to leave home. Time carries on, and the boy, now nearly a man, travels west.

Stan
On Why He Left

The corruption of city life, loneliness, and the realization that there was an alternative to it all: they were the things that sent me packing. I watched cops on lower Washington Street take money in exchange for turning a blind eye to prostitutes, drugs, and the clubs that both were coming from. Illegal gambling in pool halls was allowed to go on for the same reasons. Fire chiefs took kickbacks in return for giving promotions. This was just how it worked in the 1960s. So many of these authority figures were on the take, especially downtown.

Being around these so-called "corrupt cops," I never looked at them as the root of the problem. Over the years, I actually gained a lot of respect for them. Most of them were regular guys, trying to feed their families; good guys, doing jobs that no one else wanted, and working in a war zone for not enough money. They were left to clean up the city's mess. The cops weren't really the corrupt ones, not in my eyes; the system they worked for was. It was dirty from top to bottom.

Even at the body shop where I worked; mechanics, manager, and boss were all stealing from the company. The books were a mess, and paperwork tended to disappear. The shop did regular business with the city, which meant a lot of money. Some of that money went right back to the city, freshly laundered.

Inside my home, moral standards were high; but once I walked out the door, theft was just the way the world worked. There was little way for me to know anything else. I was soaked in it. I saw it where I worked and where I played. There was even abuse in the church where I was supposed to pray. I didn't know the word for it at the time, but it was hypocrisy. Everywhere I looked. The price tag for getting charges *of possession dropped was $300 for the judge, and $200 for the lawyer to be the middleman.*

It took me a long time to realize that the whole world didn't work this way. There were better alternatives. That was an awakening for me; understanding that I was part of the problem, and I didn't have to be. On top of that, there was this incredible loneliness of wandering on an unknown path by myself, and losing friends to heroin, the draft, or best case: family life.

What it all boils down to is: my time in the city permanently shook my faith in authority. Not the individuals, but the institutions. I think that's really what sent me in search of a place where I could live by my own rules, under my own thumb.

Chapter 3
Manson Creek

"Harmony was no more, and I felt I must find a way out of the hole. I let myself go, and dropped deeper into it."
-Stan's Journal

British Columbia, Canada. September, 1970.

It was jade, unlike anything he had ever seen. Stan had made it across the country, hopping from city to city, hostel to hostel. He had met fellow hippies, crossed the rockies, and seen redwoods in California, but this was indeed a sight. Two incredible, eleven-ton boulders of vibrant green rock were being hauled on a massive flatbed, out of a town that he hoped to find in the next hour. He pulled over to the side of the old, washed out mining road, and watched in awe as the precious rocks passed by in quantities that dwarfed his little Volkswagen. Once the mining truck passed by, Stan resumed his slow crawl up the quiet Canadian road. If the next twenty miles were anything like the last thirty, they would be slow and rocky. The Volkswagen crept along the road that was better suited for tanks than tiny hippy-mobiles.

Stan drove through the shallows of a creek. Water splashed up and around the car's rims, washing away the dust and grime of a long cross-country drive. Stan couldn't help but feel as though he had finally found what he was looking for. He imagined a place where road noise was a myth, and crime was unknown; a quiet place to settle down and learn to live off of the land. He wanted to be himself in a place where no one could tell him to do otherwise.

Ever since his last stop, in Vancouver, something had changed in him. He had been connecting the dots between cities for months, seeming to make a goodbye tour to his former life of busy streets and taller buildings. He was done connecting the big dots, and finally forging his own narrow line. Along that line, he began snowballing supplies. He attained some rope at one store, a hatchet at another. Whenever the prices were prime, he grabbed cans of beans here and there. His final shopping stop, before hitting the mining road, had been at a store that bore the sign: "Old Store, Old Guns." Stan purchased a .303 British rifle there for twenty-five dollars. To this day, it remains his smoothest, most reliable hunting weapon.

Stan's skillset was still missing an encyclopedia's worth of survival skills that he would need to last the winter. He knew how to maintain a fire for heat from his time living in the woods behind the hippy commune at the old Far Cry house; but other than that and his intricate mechanic knowledge, Stan didn't really have much to go on. Sure, he had done some fishing work back in Scituate, but that was with the help of a fifty-five foot dragger, not to mention the entire welcome mat of the Atlantic Ocean. Even once he gained these skills, they would mean very little if he couldn't manage to rent or build some kind of shelter. He knew that survival would go much like the rest of his life thus far: improvised.

Stan arrived in the town of Manson Creek, population: 22. He brought his battered car to a halt on the dirt road and stepped outside to the quiet street. Movement, other than his own, was as scarce as sound of any kind. To his right, a walkway lined with pumpkin-sized Jade boulders lead up to the front door of a quaint home. To his left stood a wooden structure, roughly the size of two RVs combined. At its side sat a single gas pump. Above that, a sign labeled "General Store" bid him enter, and he did.

The door delivered him directly to the store's checkout counter, behind which sat the owner of not only the general store, but the home with the jade-lined yard across the street. Stan was prepared for a gritty and grinless local harboring an intense disdain for an outsider. Maggie Owen was none of these things. She radiated kindness, and welcomed Stan as if he was the first guest of a party to which he had been invited.

A hospitality-fueled conversation quickly took off. Stan learned that Maggie's family had once staked a claim on Ogden Mountain, just outside of town. The claim paid off, and it was now the largest source of jade in North America. As Stan spoke with Maggie, he briefly wondered if his status as an illegal immigrant would jeopardize Maggie's welcoming attitude.

"Oh, honey, half the population here is illegal," she said. "That war of yours has people coming up in droves."

The war she spoke of was, of course, Vietnam; though it was far from Stan's war. Luckily, he wasn't actually running from the draft. In typical Stan fashion, he had found his own solution there. Although he had kept his civilian status, it didn't change the fact that he was now in Canada illegally.

Because of this influx of American immigrants, restrictions were tightening. Stan had suffered numerous defeats at multiple border checkpoints, each time being turned away for a simple reason: he was not carrying enough money. This gave him the appearance of being a vagrant, which, really, he was.

There were places along the border where only a wide ditch in a grassy field separated the two countries. There were even places where Stan could park his car, look out his window, and read Canadian license plates on the other side of the divide. Close, or not, his car could not have traversed the ditch. He had backtracked into the American border town, hoping to find another way, when the solution presented itself. It was a long, two-by-twelve board simply laying on the side of the road. Stan cut the plank it in half with his bow saw and returned to the border ditch with the large planks sticking out of the car's windows like diagonal wings. Quickly, he laid both pieces across the ditch and drove straight into Vancouver. *Welcome to Canada.*

Stan had spent a brief time there with the Hare Krishnas, playing guitar in the streets and watching the religious devotees worship. He burned every form of ID that he had, and assumed the identity of one "Stanley Joseph" from Montreal. It was a fake, temporary paper ID, and it wouldn't hold up if someone was really after him, but it was miles above nothing.

Now, many miles north in the Manson Creek general store with Maggie, Stan explained that he was hoping to build a cabin and spend the winter in town, learning what he could from the locals.

"Hey, Wally!" Maggie called to the back of the sparsely populated canned-goods aisle, and out came Stan's new best friend. The man quickly offered Stan place to stay until he could build a cabin of his own. It was that simple. These were days when anyone could wander into a city or town, talk to the nearest long-haired guy, and immediately gain a friend, a room, and in all likelihood, dinner.

Other than Maggie's family, two other distinct groups dominated the town's population; the first was illegal Americans. The second group was a family of Canadian Natives. They were fascinating to Stan. Although many people of their kind had been wiped out of cultural existence by government takeover of their lands, this family had seen through the trouble and carved out a traditional life for themselves right here in Manson Creek. Father, mother, offspring young and old, lived in one log cabin together. Stan was invited into this cabin on the second night of his stay. Refusing the invite never once crossed his mind.

Stepping inside, he witnessed a wide-open floor plan, in which the entire family resided with zero privacy. A sour, though not unpleasant smell greeted Stan at the door. His eyes quickly located the source of the scent. Instead of hanging photos on their walls, this family hung meat for drying. As he removed his boots, Stan extended a hand to the nearest wall for balance. Instead of a wall, his hand pressed firmly into an enormous moose rib cage, which was not yet completely dried.

This was a family of outstanding hunters and the walls were rarely empty. Over the course of the evening, Stan heard many stories of the casinos, bars, and hotels that the family had escaped. All of these modern amenities and commercialism were rapidly eroding the native lifestyle.

Dinner went beyond storytelling, though, and another friendship was quickly born. Soon after, he received yet another invite, this time for a moose hunt. On that hunt, the family began teaching him many of the skills that he would soon make great use of in Alaska.

Three weeks into his stay at Manson Creek, Stan's future-cabin was already two logs high. Though he gratefully took construction advice from the locals, he already knew the basics of the process from his boyhood days of playing with Lincoln Logs. The process was interrupted when opportunity knocked. Wally informed him that two men from Minnesota had arrived in town. They were in search of a living legend.

The man they were seeking, Skook Davidson, was responsible for bringing horses all the way North to the end of the Rocky Mountain

Range. He had driven a wagon train some two hundred and thirty miles above Manson Creek. There, he had a ranch where he bred and trained horses. Most of them, it was said, he let run wild.

These two Minnesotans had brought cameras, maps, packs, and a plan two years in the making, all in the hopes of finding the legendary wagoner. Initially, Stan declined the call to adventure. He had a home to build, and countless skills to learn. Yet there was perhaps no better place to learn than deep within the wilderness itself. The group of four became fast friends, and soon set out for Terminus Mountain, located at the northernmost point of the Rocky Mountain Chain. Stan would not return from this journey for four weeks, and he would get more adventure than he could have possibly imagined.

This adventure was important not for its destination, but for the survival lessons that Stan learned along the way. He travelled to the brink of the wild, then past it. There were natives that had never seen more than two white men—a minister and his pilot—ever before. Further along the way, he was passed on the hiking trail by a group of natives traveling forty miles in one day. They taught him the importance of traveling light, and bringing pack dogs for help. With those same natives, he soon learned to cope with defeat of his first, second, and third caribou hunts; then enjoyed the sweet relief of a kill on the fourth day of scouring the woods. He constructed a log raft with his travel mates, and subsequently crashed it into a logjam with devastating, unstoppable force.

That crash cost him most of his gear and food. He lived off of fireweed, eating its buds before they bloomed into beautiful purple flowers. To supplement this diet, he ate the white cambium layer of bark within spruce trees. The loss of his map taught him to travel without one. He nearly drowned in frigid waters while fording a river, and clinging to a log that he had cut into a flotation device.

All of this to meet a man beneath Terminus Mountain and shake his hand. By the end of this trip, at the age of twenty-two, Stan had learned from nature that no matter how grim the situation might be, there was always a way to pull through. This marked the beginning of Stan's lifelong motto: "Perseverance Furthers."

He had no way of knowing that in embarking on that journey, he was narrowly dodging a nightmare that had already rolled into Manson Creek.

Chapter 4
The Raid

Manson Creek, BC. October, 1971

After an all-too-long journey north, and a swift return journey by mail plane and hitchhiking, Stan completed the construction of his cabin in Manson Creek. This was where he wanted to be. The adventure had proven that. He started feeling more in tune with nature. It was a dream that lasted barely two weeks before the ever-present authorities in Stan's life came and swept it all away.

While he was away, agents of the Royal Canadian Mounted Police had come to town disguised as tourists, fishermen, and hunters. They had gotten to know the locals, and sniffed out the whereabouts of each illegal immigrant in the area. It was by stroke of luck that Stan had not been around for this investigation.

The day of the raid, another ounce of luck placed Stan on a hike, up in the mountains above his cabin. He remained unseen for the entire affair. The moment he returned to town, Wally stopped him.

"They're all gone," he said. "God, it's terrible."

"What? Who?"

"Everyone."

Now Manson Creek became another place that Stan knew held no future for him. He had avoided deportation, but it would only be a matter of time before the authorities returned and found him.

Still, he had his cabin in Manson Creek, and where else was he supposed to go for the winter? The transmission on his VW had long since broken, so if he was going anywhere, it would have to be on foot. In the end, Stan decided to risk spending the winter in Manson Creek before moving on. Where exactly he would move on to afterwards was the big question.

That quiet winter Stan gained one very important friend. A man named Steven had been living illegally in Manson Creek long enough that, before his deportation, the authorities allowed him to return to town and gather his belongings. There was one thing that Steve simply couldn't take with him, and he knew it.

Skipper was half Newfoundland Labrador and half wolf. He was big, stocky, and all black. If Steve were to return to the states with Skipper, The US border patrol would require him to visit a veterinarian, give the dog expensive shots, and sit for a thirty-day waiting period that he didn't have. Stan, on the other hand, would be spending the winter in the shell of a town, and could use the company. This was how Stan came to inherit the dog that would one day save his life.

So there sat Stan and Skipper in their cabin for the winter. The mining road was closed down for the season so the chances of a second raid were slim, not unless the RCMP rolled up in tanks and helicopters.

During this winter, Stan's bush-education continued. The natives taught him how to make snowshoes using the limited resources they had. The only tool required was a nail (used as a drill bit) and a fire bow (resembling a bow and arrow) to give it torque. Today, this device is known as a drill bow.

As his training continued, Stan learned how to gut and skin a moose. Later, a local trapper showed Stan how to set and bait traps for small game.

"The marten cycle is nothin' like lynx around here. It's long, you can't even figure it," said the old trapper.

Stan had no idea what he meant by "cycle" at the time, let alone what a marten was, but he would learn. Later in the season, Stan went for his first ride in a dog sled, as a passenger. It wasn't a practical mode of travel in Manson Creek due to the mountainous terrain, so it was a one-off experience, but one that part of him would always remember years later when taking a team of his own out into the snow. The first of those journeys was still a year and a half away. For now, he had just one dog, and one sled.

Stan often took Skipper and a light sled up the hill in his backyard on wood gathering trips. After dropping the necessary amount of lumber, Stan would push and Skipper would pull the sled-load of heat back to his cabin. More often than not Stan rode the sled, piled high with firewood, right down the mountain and to his cabin, with Skipper in the lead.

For food, Stan would join the native family on their moose hunts. Though he never shot one himself, his help in hauling the meat back to town always scored him a decent hunk of protein. This is not to say that the natives demanded Stan pull his exact weight in meat; they were very generous, as was everyone in the town.

Stan pondered his next move. By this point, he had become pretty familiar with the lifestyle in this general climate, and he began to set his sights on Alaska. Unlike most of his fellow illegal American friends, Stan wasn't running from the war, so living in the United States wouldn't be a problem. He knew he could find a place in Alaska and finally get hold of the quiet, simple lifestyle that he craved.

During that winter, two crucial letters came in carried by the Postal Service's snow cat, which was the only large vehicle capable of traversing the mining road. The first was from a girl named Charlotte. She was a Virginia girl that had been dragged all the way to Boston a few years prior by her father's short-lived job opportunity in construction. By pure and extremely fortunate happenstance, she had met Stan's younger brother. He told her of Stan's adventures, which happened to be exactly what she wanted from life. In her letter, she asked Stan to look her up if he ever found himself back in Boston, and Stan thought he just might, if the day ever came.

That day was brought sharply into focus once Stan opened the second letter. It was from the very same brother that had commenced the Stan-Charlotte connection. This letter was considerably shorter than Charlotte's, and read as follows:

"You're my best man. Better get back here."

Stan didn't much care for weddings but he wouldn't miss his brother's for all the moose meat in the world. Boston was a long trek away, but at least now Stan knew where he would be going once the snow melted.

As the weather warmed, the mining road opened, and Stan said what few goodbyes remained for him in the town. With the VW's transmission having taken a knock-out blow from a rock in the road, Stan knew that he and Skipper would be traveling by foot and thumb.

Crossing the border back into the US was complicated, thanks to

Stan's new four-legged companion. The money required to give Skipper his shots seemed like a prohibitively expensive formality, not a crucial necessity. The thirty-day wait for clearance was another problem. He simply didn't have the time. So, making a decision that Stan would consider foolish today, he opted to travel on the fringe instead.

Both man and dog hiked along the highway towards the border for a while. It was a quiet, two-lane highway with dense forest on either side. As they approached the checkpoint, Stan and Skipper ducked into the woods for a quarter mile, crossed the border, and eventually rejoined the highway on US soil. The maneuver was simple enough, except for one complication.

It was a long stretch of nothing but highway from the border, so if a patrol car happened to drive by, it would be thoroughly obvious that any hitchhiker moving away from the checkpoint had found a way around it. Where else could he be coming from? Stan was praying to get a ride before border patrol drove by. Sure enough, the latter came first.

"Where are you coming from?" asked the border agent.

"Oh," Stan started, "I got a ride to the border but they turned me away."

"You're American?"

"Yeah, but the problem wasn't with me. They said I had to go back to town and get my dog a bunch of shots or something. Do you know anything about that?"

The border agent did, and gave Stan some pretty detailed instructions on how he could get into Canada. The agent even went as far as recommending a specific veterinarian.

"Thanks," said Stan. "Can't believe I walked all the way up for nothing."

The border agents wished him good luck and went on their way, back towards the border. Stan's momentary celebration of his victorious fib was cut short. All it would take was for those agents to return to the checkpoint and mention in passing the man and dog they had encountered on the road. Next, Stan wondered if they had a radio in their car. Could they already be double-checking his story? He started walking faster and debated another quick dart back into the forest.

He heard the river-like whoosh of an approaching car at his back and immediately knew they were on to him. They must have done a u-turn, and now they were going to apprehend him. As Stan was coming to terms with the fact that he would be missing his brother's wedding, he turned to see that the vehicle was in fact, civilian. He stuck out his thumb. The driver pulled over, and Stan and Skipper made their getaway.

Over the course of a couple weeks, they hitched cross-country back to Boston. It was good to be going home, but Stan knew he wouldn't stay long. Alaska was on his mind.

<u>Stan</u>

On The Final Leap Into Alaska

This part of my life was incredibly focused. I was on a mission. Finally, a good, meaningful life was within my reach. Nothing in my control was going to keep me from the Alaskan Bush.

I was never a planner; always a fly by the seat of my pants kind of guy. Still, I didn't rush a single thing. The dream would happen, but only if I took it a careful inch at a time.

Of course I was excited, but excitement felt like a distraction, which I tried to keep to a minimum. I even did my best to avoid talking to others about what I was going to do. It's not that I was being secretive. I was proud. But for some reason, blabbing about the whole adventure seemed to take energy away from it. Talking about a goal seemed to satisfy the urge that had me pushing towards it in the first place. This is a rule that I continue to live by to this day.

Chapter 5
The Leap

Boston. November, 1972.

Tonight the old boat yard outside of Boston was quiet, and about as cold as winter could muster. Two years had passed since Stan lived here in a dry docked boat that was going nowhere. It had been his last place of residence before picking up and traveling west in search of a greener skyline.

He stepped up to an old steam pipe, glanced around briefly, and reached into the warm, moist air. He pulled out two solid oak sticks and examined them. They were coming along nicely. The bend was almost where he needed it. Sorting out the weave pattern would still be difficult, but he would cross that bridge once he came to it; the extra hassle was well worth the money saved. Snowshoes were expensive, and Stan was making them for next to nothing.

The Canadian natives had shown him more than a few tricks on the crafting of snowshoes, but those had involved bending spruce branches into the outer frame and weaving a mesh out of wet moose hide string, known as babish. In Boston, no such materials existed. Stan had heard of shaping wood by the process of steaming, but he had never tried it before. Now, it appeared to be working.

Every waking hour of that winter was spent preparing for the final departure into the Alaskan wild. Stan quickly recovered his old job at the body shop. When he punched out, he would go straight to either crafting gear or gathering supplies. He was going. That was certain; this brief return to Boston was his last stop.

His brother's wedding had come and gone without complete

catastrophe, although it was a high-class affair and Stan's ponytail was not on the guest list. Stan's mother had briefly chased him around the house brandishing a pair of scissors as part of a larger plot against him. He thought it ironic that the woman who had told him to not run with scissors all his life was doing exactly that. After evading capture, Stan agreed to a compromise; he would keep his hair and in return, agree to wear a tuxedo for the wedding, but not a moment longer.

Throughout the proceedings, there was much talk of "Stanley coming out of the forest," and, "Stanley bringing a live wolf back with him." He tried to talk about the things he had seen and the adventures he had, but never quite felt he could do them justice. Manson Creek and Boston were separate realities, impossible to reconcile.

He had been planning to depart for Alaska only weeks after his brother's wedding and improvise a journey all the way to Alaska. As luck would have it, forming a proper plan and finding a car of his own became a necessity after he made one crucial stop.

The Massachusetts Society for the Prevention of Cruelty to Animals was a caged jungle. It was inhabited by rabbits with broken legs, birds that could not fly, and others of fur or scales that had suffered abuse. The purpose of this visit, though, was not to visit the animals.

A twenty-one year old girl named Charlotte worked at the shelter. She had written Stan months prior while he was still in Manson Creek. Stan thought it best to show up at her place of work, as he had been warned about her father's disdain for hippies.

They walked amongst the animals, small talking about the various canines and felines. Charlotte showed Stan her small, orphaned group of baby squirrels, which she had made herself personally responsible for mothering until they were mature enough to be released again. Charlotte had known about Stan's plans to run off to Alaska, though she made no commitment to join him that day.

The two became friends and soon it was official that Stan and Skipper would have a female travel companion for their great adventure. In the beginning, Charlotte was simply a partner in the journey. Both had a fascination with wildlife, and neither was interested in working an office job or living in an apartment. They were bonded platonically over their interest in living among the trees. Relationships like that do have a way of evolving, though, and after a few months, the two became lovers.

Life made an eerie return to the old ways for a while. Stan moved back in with his parents and continued to work at the body shop. There was one crucial difference between this phase of Stan's life and his childhood; Stan knew exactly where he was going. He wasn't just working to make ends meet. Instead, he was gathering the funding that would kick-start the rest of his life.

He and Charlotte would need a tent, tools, ammunition, and a car to get them where they were going. Preparation was a frugal process that took most of the winter. Wherever they could, Stan and Charlotte cut corners, opting to borrow and craft rather than purchase. For the snowshoes, once the oak wood was successfully steamed and bent, Stan had to find a way to weave them together. The Canadian natives had shown him the proper cross-pattern using moose hide, but it was a process so quick and second-natured to them that it went completely over Stan's head. So one night he headed down to the to the main shopping drag on Washington Street, well after the stores had closed. He found an adventure supply store and there, hanging in the front window, was exactly what he needed.

Stan removed his winter gloves, produced a pen and paper, and copied down the intricate pattern of the snowshoe's web. From his notes, he was able to reproduce the design using nylon rope. The result was a one-of-a-kind set of Boston-grade, birch and nylon snowshoes. Stan proudly eyed them, and let his imagination wander to images of Charlotte, himself, and Skipper traversing vast and vacant spruce tree forests.

Transportation to that land of deep snow was the next obstacle they were faced with. Buying a new car would have been an inconceivable waste. They had little money, Stan was a well-seasoned mechanic, and they would most likely be abandoning the vehicle once they hit the tree line. In the end, Stan got his hands on a '64 Chevy Station Wagon. It burned through oil like a wildfire and barely had an ounce of life left in its bones.

Nightly on the street outside of his parent's home, Stan touched cold fingers to colder metal, gradually resuscitating the car. He gave the pistons new rings and re-honed each of the six cylinders. Fortunately, Stan was experienced with this kind of work, so the job required little time, and zero retries.

For the last addition to the car Stan purchased three spare tires, as he knew they would be going far, and likely on rough terrain. He had left a lot of valuable survival gear in Manson Creek, so before they hit Alaska they would have to traverse the same washed-out mining road on which he had seen the jade boulders, one year prior.

Meanwhile, Charlotte was having a great deal of difficulty concealing her activities from her father. She was planning to run away from home, and couldn't keep it a secret for long. Around December, she moved in with Stan's parents; in a separate bedroom, of course. These were the 70s and the couple was out of wedlock.

Skipper was fitting in with the family very well. His inner wolf caused him to only respect those that could physically best him. Stan had already succeeded in a playful wrestling match, and gained a loyal and docile companion. The future homesteader was worried that other members of his family would be held to the same wolf-pack standard. He once came home to find Skipper motionless, staring fixedly at a block of cheese that was resting on the arm of his mother's armchair. She had settled down for her customary glass of wine and evening of TV. Skipper remained a statue, even after Stan had entered.

"Ok," said Stan's mother, and Skipper lunged for it. As the dog's jaws worked, and his teeth chomped, Stan asked his mother how she managed to pull that one off. She shrugged the question off. "I raised you."

In February of '73, the supplies were gathered, the car was rolling, and the excitement was electric. The original intention was to stay in Boston and depart once the spring sun started shining; but, as young couples are wont to do, they gave in to their eager hearts.

Stan could barely handle himself. His mind, always a few steps ahead, was already constructing a new cabin. The car was loaded and running when his mother said something to him that would stick forever.

"We don't ever need to see you again. If you never come back, that's fine. As long as you're happy." Regardless of how crazy or harebrained the idea of running off to middle-of-nowhere Alaska was, the fiery Irish woman knew it was better than seeing Stan stagnate in Boston. In her mind, it was miracle enough that he had escaped the collapse that heroin had brought. By now she had a firm idea of all that city life had done to him, and how close he had come to becoming a career criminal. She couldn't risk letting him fall back into the mess, even if it meant she would never see her son again.

The first time she told Stan those words, he took it to mean that she loved him even more than herself. The seventh and eight times, through pay phones and letters, he wondered if maybe she just wanted a quieter home.

In late February of 1973, Stan, his girlfriend Charlotte, and their dog Skipper headed west. They had five hundred dollars to their names, and a car that was so packed with gear that Charlotte sat on a stack of spare tires all the way across the country. She made no complaints, though. She was right where she wanted to be.

Crossing the border into Canada was much easier this time around; they had enough money. To the border patrol, they were just another American couple on their way to Alaska. No problem there.

Then came the drive upward along that lone, rough, road that would take them into Manson Creek. There were a lot of valuables waiting for them; a nice tin stove, a gun, some extra nonperishables; all useful things Stan wasn't willing to drag back to Boston on foot.

They arrived at the mouth of the road to find it a closed down, snow-covered mess. They were only fifty miles from Manson Creek, but that was as far as the station wagon would take them. The snowshoes were about to be put to the test.

Cold conditions and hard walking were a shock to Charlotte. Snowshoeing is not an easy way to travel, especially compared to sitting in a warm car. There was some crying involved on that first day, and once the sun fell, the couple only had two miles under their belts. *Forty-eight to go...*

The next morning, though, Charlotte awoke with a steely look of determination. She loved what they were doing, even though it was difficult. Their pace quadrupled the next day, and the crying ceased. Again, their speed doubled, and laughter began. Soon, walking on the snow's surface was second nature, and they arrived in Manson Creek.

Snowshoeing back to the car with a stove strapped to their backs would be less than ideal. Fortunately, they had another option. The Canadian Postal Service utilized a heavy, tracked snowcat to deliver mail to the tiny town once every thirty days during the winter months. This meant Stan and Charlotte had some time to cool their heels in Manson Creek before hopefully hitching a ride back to the station wagon.

There was more to this place than equipment, though, and soon after arriving, Stan gave a one-two knock on an old familiar cabin. The door opened, and out poured that sour scent of dry meat. The native family was thrilled to see that Stan had found love, as well as a compass to guide his life. He showed them the shoes he had made, and thanked them for teaching him the process in the first place.

They had some fun during their visit. In Stan's absence, the natives had purchased a snow machine—also known as snow mobile or snowgo depending on place of residence. It had no practical use for them, as they preferred to hunt on foot. It was, however, a great theme park ride. They would take turns firing up the two-stroke engine, and immediately pegging it to full throttle. The machine would scream and take off in a straight line, often cat-walking up on its hind end, until it either rolled or crashed into a tree.

Eventually, the snowcat arrived. They made a deal with the driver, loaded all of the gear into the cat, and cruised back to the station wagon in style.

On April 1st, 1973, Stan and Charlotte left Canada and entered Alaska. That was the day that the plan ended and the improvising began. They knew what they wanted, but had no idea how to get it. Purchasing a plot of land off the grid would be ideal, but even in that best case scenario, traveling to said place would present a whole different challenge. If they couldn't find legal land, Stan and Charlotte were prepared to drive the station wagon to the end of the longest road they could find, abandon it, haul everything they had into the woods, and build a cabin there.

They hit Fairbanks and immediately started asking around. The locals informed them that there were a few large plots of federal land that had just opened up. They would simply have to find their spot, submit a form, build a home, and place a waterproof jar containing the deed on the edge of their property in order to own a five-acre plot of land. That was the good information. The bad information: they were advised to build a boat and float down the Tanana River to find their spot. Someone who must have been making up his advice as he went along informed them that river water was too shallow near Fairbanks, so they would have to move their heaviest gear down river to the village of Minto and pick it up on the way by.

So began the process of gathering final supplies and shuttling them to Minto. On their first run into the village, Stan noted how modern the housing seemed to be. It was far from the rustic settlement he had expected. He would later learn that the expanding banks of the Tanana River had recently forced the government to spend a great deal of money moving all of the residents further inland.

In Minto, Stan met an Alaskan Native by the name of Lloyd Charlie. Lloyd was a hunter, trapper, and dog musher by winter. During the summer, he did construction work. It was a customary practice in the area; work during the summer, live by tradition in the winter. As per the broadly accepted sentiment of the times, Stan and Charlotte were invited into Lloyd's home for food and conversation.

Within Lloyd's home, he passed the young couple a basket of something he called "Indian Crackers." They were large, round, and hardy sort of crackers. Stan thought it possible that their ingredients might have included a hint of cement. Lloyd explained that they were a traditional native food that was baked right there in Minto. It would be months before Stan came across his first mass-produced box of Sailor Boy Pilot Bread, and realized that Lloyd had been messing with him. Lloyd had a sense of humor, and this kept the two in touch for years to come.

His comic nature was outmatched only by his generosity. He had a one-year-old pup on his team that didn't seem to have a knack for racing. Rather than sell the pup to another musher, Lloyd simply gave him to Stan, suspecting he might need another dog. By this point, Stan had yet to drive a dog team of his own, but any dog's ability to pack weight made them invaluable hiking partners. They named the small blonde pup Minto, and he became the second member of what would soon be Stan's first dog team.

After tea and "Indian Crackers," Stan and Charlotte found a place in Minto to store their heavy supplies while they built a boat in Fairbanks.

These days, they were still living out of the station wagon and sleeping in a parking lot in Fairbanks. It's difficult to say where Stan and Charlotte would have wound up if they had actually gone through with their boat plan. Luckily, five days into their stay in Fairbanks, they picked up a hitchhiker who set them on the proper course. He explained that air travel was a completely different animal in Alaska as opposed to the lower forty-eight. He told them about trappers being brought out to the bush by small charter planes and being picked up two months later.

"They'll drop you off anywhere you want to go," he said.

So they returned to Minto, now tasked with hauling all of their supplies back to Fairbanks. The hitchhiker welcomed them to stay in his home for the next couple days while they put their car up for sale and picked up their final odds and ends. Before Stan and Charlotte left the hitchhiker's company, he would give them one final piece of information that proved to be invaluable. He told them if they ever wound up near the village of Tanana, to look up his friend, Joe Runyon. Mr. Runyon would later go on to be one of Stan's most important contacts in the village nearest his homestead. The simple act of picking up a hitchhiker had altered the course of Stan and Charlotte's lives for the better.

Eventually, a college student took them up on the car, and after the purchase, brought them straight the airport. Stan and Charlotte pocketed the money from the car sale and planned to put it directly into a charter flight. They would go from wheels, to wings, to boots; all in the course of one day. Once they arrived at the charter office, though, they were met with some resistance.

Another homesteading couple had been rescued only ten days prior, having nearly starved to death after a year in the woods. That couple, the Kellers, had been dropped off by a charter flight from the same company. They were expecting another supply drop months later. Instead, the pilot lost track of where he had left them, their supplies never arrived, and they barely made it through the winter with their lives. It was a big scare in the bush pilot community. Many were worried about lawsuits, bad reputations, and losing their pilot licenses.

"Where do you want to go?" asked the charter coordinator from behind the desk. "You have to have a destination."

Stan had no idea how to answer the question. It was a decision he had been planning to make from the air. Out came the map, and then came another life changing decision. The Tozitna River was represented by a narrow, winding blue line, flowing directly into the Yukon River. Other than that identifier, the area was far from any other words on the map.

"Anywhere in this valley," Stan ran his finger along the Tozitna.

"What kind of experience do you have?"

This could be answered with a little more clarity. Stan told him that he had lived in British Columbia, he had a gun, and could shoot a moose. That was enough, barely. Stan still seemed a little greenhorn. There's only so much that a skinny 23-year-old can do to convince someone that he's a hardy survivor. The flight was approved and the cargo was loaded onto the plane. The charter coordinator offered Stan one last piece of advice:

"Shoot anything that moves."

This was something that the Kellers had been morally opposed to doing, and naturally it caused them a few problems. Charlotte and Stan, on the other hand, had every intention of hunting, trapping, and eating meat during their stay.

They would be flying to their new home in a Helio Courier. These were the perfect aircraft for this purpose because they could take off and land in a short stretch. The plane could have carried a thousand pounds, but since no one knew exactly where they would be landing, Stan and Charlotte had to keep their baggage under six hundred. With this news, Stan took the heaviest, least useful items, packaged them up, and mailed them to the to the post office nearest to their landing site, in the village of Tanana. Three days later, the Tanana postmaster would strain his back lifting a mechanic's toolbox and sledgehammer that was addressed to a stranger named Stan Zuray.

On April 9th, 1973, Charlotte, Skipper, Minto, and Stan took flight with their supplies, heading northwest from Fairbanks. It would be five years before Stan saw the city again.

<u>Stan</u>

On the Point of No Return

I've never liked planes, probably because I'm not the one driving them. I don't even like being given rides in dog sleds, or snow machines. My plane ride to the Tozi River Valley was my second time in a plane, but my first ever landing (I had gone skydiving once before).

Yes, the trip was crazy, and all three of us worried about crashing on one of those snowdrifts. Knowing the Tozi River as I do now, it was insane to even attempt a landing where we eventually set down.

Way more worrisome than that, though, was the prospect of turning back to Fairbanks, and landing on concrete.

Chapter 6
The Landing

Their pilot was trembling with nerves. When it came to flying Helio Couriers into the bush, he had a passable amount of experience. He wasn't much older than the young homesteaders he was carrying. Though he was a bonafide pilot, that didn't make the landing conditions any friendlier.

Stan, sitting co-pilot, was experiencing a similar set of nerves. His eyes were fixated on the passing landscape below. Though it was already April, the land still sported many thick patches of snow. Lakes were frozen through with solid blue ice, and rivers had only just begun to show signs of melt. The grass and weeds in the meadows below remained brown from the waterless winter freeze. It was the healthy population of spruce trees that gave the land its patches of green. Stan had seen similar lands in Canada, but never from this gorgeous perspective.

They flew up and down the Tozitna river valley, looking for a stretch of river or lake large enough to touch down on. The lakes would have been preferable, as they allowed the most length for takeoff, landing, and an easy turn around with no risk of clipping wings on a tree branch. The one downside to the lakes was that they were mostly covered in wave after wave of dense snowdrift, all of which the plane's landing gears would have to crash through.

The pilot weighed his options, and opted to try for a lake landing. He drew closer and closer to the icy surface. The landing gear clipped through two or three waves of snow, causing the plane to buck and twist. He quickly pulled up, likely wishing he could just turn around and return to Fairbanks. The engine groaned in disapproval as the packed Courier climbed back to safety.

Two more lake landings were attempted; each time the plane was forced skyward. The truth was simple: lakes would not be working for them, not today. The search for a long stretch of river commenced.

"How about here?" the pilot's voice buzzed into Stan's headphones with a mere fraction of its natural fidelity, successfully concealing how uncomfortable he was with the whole idea of dropping a plane on the aforementioned section of river.

Stan looked below, pretending to size-up the location, checking to see if it fit his imaginary criteria. "Looks good."

The pilot took on an approach pattern, zigging and zagging the Helio Courier in the vicinity of the landing zone, gradually dropping altitude all the while. On the final approach, his trusty piloting instincts naturally took over and the plane, in fact, did not tumble into a wrecked ball of people, dogs, and other homesteader possessions. They had made it to solid ice, right on top of the Tozitna River.

Stan and Charlotte took to unloading their gear while the pilot paced around, voicing his concerns about the take off he would soon be performing. The supply load came off in no time. It wasn't much: two dogs, some tarps, a thirty dollar tent, stove, axe, bow saw, two sleeping bags, some clothing, flour, rice, soybeans, brown beans, a guitar, a shotgun, a .303 British, a .22, and a suitcase full of ammo.

"Hey, so where are we?" Stan asked, and the map came out.

The pilot spread the chart out on the plane's tail wing. Now it was his turn to pretend.

"Here, we're right on this river bend."

It would be a month before anyone came to realize it, but the pilot had just made the same mistake that left the Kellers stranded. In this case, it was an error less fatal and more inconvenient. Stan and Charlotte weren't expecting to see another plane bringing more supplies anytime soon. They had flown out with all they owned.

The pilot was so anxious to get going that he almost took off without taking his payment. Stan handed him his $200, then retreated back to a safe distance and watched with Charlotte as the plane turned, climbed, and disappeared into the sky.

The plane's engine fought a steady losing battle against the incredible silence that was waiting for Stan and Charlotte, and soon they were left with only the sounds of the wind. They set up their tent, built a small fire, and ate their first ration of beans and rice on the Tozitna River. They climbed into their respective sleeping bags, and Charlotte closed her eyes right away. Stan, on the other hand, lay wide-awake, fired up like a coal burner.

"Hey, tomorrow we should put packs on the dogs."

"I know, Stan." Charlotte's eyes remained shut.

"And probably head north east for a good ways."

"Sounds good."

"Definitely want to pack light, though."

"Stan, can we talk about this in the morning?"

He took the hint and turned down his volume for the night, though it would still be a few hours before his mind finally allowed him to sleep. He gazed up at the dark sky, catching glimpses of stars between the high-flying clouds, and wondered if there was any place better than this one.

Morning finally came. They packed and set out for their expedition, leaving ninety percent of their supplies behind in order to travel light. The goal was to find a picture to match a simple phrase: *Living in the mountains.* It was a romantic, Alaskan-sounding string of words, and so, after passing through a nice, grassy grove of monstrous seventy-foot tall spruce trees, they were well on their way to the Ray Mountain range.

The snow was deep in places, and the necessity of snowshoeing slowed them down a great deal. Towards the end of the second day of hiking, they entered the foothills. A few steep climbs only further took the wind out of their sails. Both Stan and Charlotte realized it would be adding weeks of work to choose a homestead so far from their landing. Although this was to be their home for all time, how could they let lethargy stand between them and their perfect spot in the mountains?

As they climbed, the trees became sparse, and their supply of food grew thin. Stan found himself wondering how exactly he would make a log cabin without any logs. He was forced to shoot ravens out of the trees for what little meat they provided. The meat itself, once prepared over an open fire, was somewhat tough and had the strong taste of spruce trees. It wasn't ideal, but Stan had a way of finding enjoyment in anything that served its purpose of filling his stomach.

It took about three ravens before the young couple realized that they had walked past the perfect homestead just ten minutes from the landing. It had trees for a cabin, even ground, and was located near the Tozitna River, which would hopefully yield fish in the summer.

During the return journey, they came across a large, dark shape, sitting in the woods before them. Of all things, it was a cabin, already built. The odds of such a discovery were slim beyond visibility, but there it was. The structure had a low roof and seemed to be made entirely of dead, half rotten trees. Both Stan and Charlotte theorized that it had been abandoned for decades. Stan called out, but heard no answer.

They approached the cabin, only to see in greater detail how much its structure had deteriorated. Inside the dark building, they came across a tape recorder. If the cabin hadn't been left to rot decades prior, then why was it in such poor condition?

Stan and Charlotte pressed play on the recorder, and the sound of a woman's voice crackled into the abandoned cabin. She described a grim situation of diminished food and near hopelessness. It quickly became apparent that they were standing in the former cabin of Mr. and Mrs. Keller. The tape continued to play as Stan and Charlotte poked around the cabin, and a story unfolded.

The Kellers were hippies, far more so than Stan and Charlotte could ever claim to be. They had been told by their guru that the Ray Mountain range was the third eye of Alaska, and that was where they should live to become one with nature.

They were vegetarians, and refused to kill anything; this included trees. Hence, the cabin was made entirely of dead and rotting wood. This deathless lifestyle continued for a month and a half, until they realized that their pilot would not be returning. As their one month cache of food dwindled, they made one exception to their rule. They had a dog that needed to be fed, and not enough food to share. For humane reasons, they were forced to shoot a moose. All of the meat was given to their dog, though. Their thinking was, as the madness of being a carnivore consumed the dog, they would remain pure, and eventually nurse him back to mental stability.

Stan and Charlotte realized that the Kellers were not the most pragmatic people in Alaska. They had assembled elaborate, artful flooring made of tiny stones, yet hadn't installed a door in their cabin. Rather than turn their barrel into a functioning stove, they cut it open and made it into an open fireplace. Unfortunately, their chimney was so short, it didn't draft, and Stan and Charlotte couldn't warm up the cabin without smoking it out. That night, they had to sleep outside.

Finally returning to the landing site, they took a few days to move all of their supplies up to the spruce grove and set up a nicer, more permanent camp. They wrapped a tarp around four trees, and draped another over top for a roof. This tarp fortress became their temporary cook shack and hang out area. Around and inside it were snowshoes, dog sled, harnesses, and everything of value. This was the very structure that would soon burn to the ground.

Then came the exploring. Based on the location that the pilot had indicated on their map, both went off in one direction looking for a lake, hoping to score some ducks, but the lake didn't exist. Another time, they struck out to find a creek and instead found a lake in its place. This was how they slowly came to realize that they had no idea where they were.

<u>Stan</u>
On Tanana

They say no man is an island. While some may come close, I did not. The tools, guns, dogs, food, and lessons I was given were all key to my survival. Many of these things came from Tanana. Practical stuff aside, the friendships and memories I have gained from this place are priceless.

The giving continues to this day, and I hope that I have been able to give some back, now that I have my feet firmer on the ground.

<u>Chapter 7</u>
Finding Tanana

Their one-month supply of food had taken them nearly that far. The village of Tanana was supposedly some forty miles south of where they had been dropped off. Whether or not that assessment still held true remained to be seen. Like it or not, it was time to head into town, officially stake the land, and hopefully buy some food. On May 1st, three weeks after they landed on the Tozi River, Stan left Charlotte with the dogs for protection and headed south with his pack and snowshoes, hoping to find the village.

He knew that if he crossed the open flats, he had a good chance of hitting the right valley. That valley would then meet up with the Allakaket Trail and hopefully, lead him right into Tanana. He also knew that it was impossible for him to go too far. The Yukon River would stop him before that point.

The hiking wasn't bad, though constant changes in snow's consistency kept Stan switching between snowshoes and boots. He crossed through a forest of thin, young spruce trees, and eventually came out into open country. The ground was nothing but tussocks, and apart from the occasional patch of trees, was wide open in all directions. This was an area that Stan would later come to know as the Tozi flats.

At the end of the flats, Stan entered what seemed to be an older, or perhaps just richer forest. He encountered a creek, and opted to remain within its valley, which was heading roughly south. By this point, a vague path became apparent, and Stan grew more and more confident that he was on his way to Tanana.

The forest broke, and Stan began a slight uphill climb through sparse land that resembled the Tozi flats. Once he reached the top of that mountain, known to Tanana locals as 14-mile hill, he beheld something he didn't quite expect.

It was a massive, vertical, white square, towering above the distant trees. Stan had been walking for ten hours at this point. He rubbed his eyes clean to get a better glimpse at the object. It looked like a drive-in movie screen. He didn't know much of anything about Tanana at the time, but thought it odd that the town was a big enough destination that it required a thirty-story hotel. As he drew closer, he saw that there were more than a couple of these huge man-made structures. The existence of a skyline on the Yukon River was enough food for thought to carry Stan right up to his destination.

What he ended up walking into was an air force base. There were a couple of large structures with tin siding, water tanks, fuel tanks, and a wide-open parking lot. It was much more developed than anything he could have expected. The tall, white structures that he had seen from 14-mile hill were sending/receiving dishes for the Air Force's White Alice program. This base was a "DEW Line Site," which stood for Distant Early Warning. Essentially, it was an electronic version of Paul Revere, poised to shout, "The Russians are Coming!" The Tanana locals referred to it as "The Site," for short. Stan walked up to the base and knocked on one of the doors, which quickly swung open.

"Hi," said Stan. "Can you tell me which way to Tanana?"

The man on the other side of the door looked at the young boy with utter confusion. They were ten miles outside of Tanana, and as far as he knew, there wasn't another village for sixty miles. If you were traveling on foot, you didn't just know how to find Tanana; you lived there. Now here was this kid, speaking with a thick Boston accent, seemingly out for a stroll in the Alaskan wilderness, and asking for directions.

"Where the hell are you coming from?"

That was the beginning of a long relationship between Tozi Homesteaders and The Site. After a brief chat over coffee in the commons area of the base, Stan was given a ride down the ten-mile stretch of dirt road, and into the village of Tanana. It was a quaint yet proud little town that sat perched right along the banks of the Yukon River. Stan started his day at the post office, where he picked up the sledge hammer and toolbox that had been shipped in nearly one month prior. He wasn't planning on hauling the tools back to his homestead this trip, but knew he had to get them out of the post office before they were returned to sender.

Next he mailed the form that would officially stake his claim on the land that he and Charlotte were currently living on. While there, he asked about the name that the hitchhiker had provided him, and after some detective work, he found the home of Joe Runyon. His first encounter with Joe was almost a carbon copy of that with Lloyd Charlie, minus the Indian Crackers and plus a couple of dogs. Joe was friendly, welcoming, and curious to hear about what Stan was doing way out on the Tozitna River. Stan, in turn, was curious about the land, the village, and its customs. He asked about hunting and fishing, and Joe Runyon told him what he knew.

After a good night's rest in Joe's home, Stan was given a ride back up to The Site. He had to hit the trail and get home to Charlotte. The original plan was to beg, borrow or steal a children's snow-sled to drag the supplies home, but the total haul had grown to two hundred pounds worth of assorted necessities. It was a little much for even the sturdiest of play sleds. Making it home on foot simply wouldn't be an option.

Fortunately, Joe Runyon agreed to hold Stan's tools and sledge hammer, and did him one better. He gave Stan three of his dogs and a sled to complete his return journey.

"Just scream like hell to get them to go, yell 'Gi' if you want them to turn right, 'Haw' if you want them to turn left," said Joe, and so concluded his training session on how to drive a team. Stan gave thanks and nervously gripped the sled's handles. Then, for the first time, he yelled "UH-kay!" The dogs were off. They were Cleetsa, Monk, and Rocky.

With the weight he was hauling, three dogs were barely enough to keep the sled moving. Stan wound up kicking and pushing a great deal more than he initially expected. Still, despite the two hundred extra pounds, Stan made it back to Charlotte in just thirteen hours, as opposed to the eleven it had taken him to hike into town empty handed.

Charlotte was elated with Stan's return. While Stan was gone, she was having an adventure all of her own, spending the first night in the cabin alone for miles in all directions. She hadn't been quick to fear, though it was still a mental hurdle that needed jumping. Now, Stan was back one day early, with more than she had expected.

All they had hoped for was some food and clear sense on how to find civilization. Acquiring three dogs was far beyond icing on the cake; it was another cake altogether. Cleetsa, Monk, and Rocky met Skipper and Minto without any undue violence and quickly formed into a pack with Skipper at the top of the hierarchy. Now Stan and Charlotte not only had a healthy force of guardians, they had their first dog team.

After a few weeks, once the trees thawed and were ready to be debarked, construction of the cabin was underway. It was two logs high when Stan and Charlotte heard the familiar droll of an outboard motor approaching. Its driver was a man named Ringo Mclaughlan. His passenger was his wife, Janie. They had heard from a friend at The Site that some twenty-three year old kid and his girlfriend were settling into life along the upper Tozitna River. Ringo regularly spent time along lower parts of the Tozi, so he had decided to push his boat further up river through to shallower waters, in the hopes of meeting said "crazy young couple."

Stan waved The Mclaughlans down and welcomed them up to his incomplete home. They talked about hunting and trapping, and briefly small talked over their mutual friends from The Site. Stan asked how the trip up had been. The answer to this was more important than mere small talk. If the traveling was good and the water was deep, it meant Stan and Charlotte had a faster, easier means of getting supplies to the cabin during the summer. As it turned out, the water was approaching its highest, and that wasn't very high at all. Ringo and Janie had scraped bottom a few times on their way up, but had taken no serious damage. They expected maybe one more trip would be possible before the water was too shallow to be traveled upon.

"Is there anything you need from town?" Ringo offered.

"If you're coming up anyway," Stan said. "I'd be happy to pay you to bring a few sacks of flour with you." They still had some money to offer, and although Stan had just gotten back from town, he knew they would soon have to make another trip. Hunting, farming, and any form of subsistence living wouldn't begin in earnest until the cabin itself was complete. They needed a long-term solution for food.

"Sorry, no can do," said Ringo. "I don't do work for hire. I can maybe grab you a loaf of bread or something."

Stan knew they needed far more, but dropped the subject and accepted what Ringo offered. By evening, Ringo and Janie were on their way, and the work continued around the homestead. That night,

Charlotte entered the cook shack to prepare dinner on the stove that would soon burn almost everything they owned to ash.

Chapter 8
The Fire, Continued

The hot orange blaze brought each tree's branches crashing down within an hour. Once the ammunition died down, Stan and Charlotte ran back up the riverbank, and commenced kicking out the many brush fires that had cropped up since their retreat. It was an important custodial task in a forest that, though speckled with snow, could flare up again and burn for acres all around.

With each of the trees charred and stripped of their branches, the tower of flames vanished. The sun was high now, and would remain so until 10 pm that night. Thin ghosts of white smoke drifted up from the remains of the couple's homesteading dream. Through sleepless eyes, Stan and Charlotte searched the area for any possessions that remained. There were a few tools that had been lying over by the partially constructed cabin. As far as clothing went, Stan had a pair of dress pants, moccasins, and the underwear he had on during the fire. The arsenal was down to one rifle, Stan's .303, which had been in the pup tent with him.

Stan had already constructed a food cache up in a cluster of trees, but it held only one sack of dog food. The rest was in the fire. A plastic bucket of soybeans had melted inward, producing a hardened mold of charred beans and plastic. Stan cracked the blackened shell, and found four handfuls of beans that had been burned, but untainted by plastic.

All of the pots and pans that they grabbed from the Kellers' cabin were reduced to puddles of aluminum. The tin stove was riddled with holes from the flying bullet casings that went off in the fire.

Stan and Charlotte knew there was no way they could make it through the rest of the summer with what they had, let alone winter.

They now planned a week to hunt down more food, then walk the thirty miles back to town with everything they could carry. They hadn't moved here to be beggars, and didn't want to arrive in town with empty stomachs. Once in Tanana, they would look for work, even if it meant returning to Fairbanks. The dream was dead merely two months after it started.

Stan went around in his dress pants and moccasins, shooting beavers with his .303, which was significantly over-powered for the job. For dog food, he marched up and down the river, catching grayling, which are similar to trout. This only yielded a few meals. Soon they resorted to mixing burned beans with dog food, grinding them up, adding water, and cooking them into little burger patties.

One week after the fire, Stan heard Ringo's boat making its approach. As he pulled up to the homestead, he was likely surprised to see Stan's choice in attire. No shirt, thin slacks, and moccasins weren't exactly typical bush-wear. Then again, when out in the wilderness, a man was free to dress as he pleased.

Ringo had brought a friend of his, and a future friend of Stan's named Joe Darbishire. The boat seemed to be riding lower than normal, in waters that had only grown more shallow since Ringo's last visit. It was carrying far more than two people. Though Ringo had turned Stan down on his request to purchase food from town, here sat his boat loaded down with, literally, five hundred pounds of food, absolutely free. He had raided The Site's storeroom of its surplus and expired foods, and made the sketchy trip up river exclusively to help Stan and Charlotte achieve their dream. He had no idea how much he would actually be helping.

From their landing on the riverbank, Ringo and Joe couldn't see the wreckage of Stan's camp. As they walked up, Stan gave him the sugarcoated telling of the past week's events.

"Oh, we had a few problems. Ya know?"

They crested the bank and Ringo saw what little there was left. His first two words would have been anyone's.

"Holy shit," he said. "You burned out."

Right then and there, Ringo's friend Joe removed his leather boots and gave them to Stan. It was a swift and silent gesture. Before Stan could even start to decline, Joe insisted that he had a pair of hip-waders and could easily wear them home.

That was the turning point. Stan and Charlotte realized that they had a chance. With the food they were given, they could keep up the fight, finish the cabin, and get back on their feet before winter.

Ringo wasn't the last of the help they saw, either. He went back to town with a mental list of everything the young homesteaders were short of, and word of the loss spread like a flood. Later that summer, a crazy ex-race car driver that now worked at The Site named Dale "Crash" Thompson, flew his plane over the cabin and dropped a .22 rifle, some bug spray and a package full of other odds and ends, including a shirt for Stan. The generosity of people like Ringo, Joe, and Crash pulled Stan and Charlotte through their summer crisis. The winter, however, was an entirely different bridge that would soon need crossing. They had work to do and lessons to learn before they would be ready for the cold.

<u>Stan</u>
On the Draft

The fact that I managed to live the life I did can be credited to many things. Even so far in my story, the friendly people I met helped a great deal. Luck took me a good ways further. There was one other fork in the road, way earlier, that came very close to preventing my adventure from ever starting.

Vietnam and the draft, then and to this day, hold a conflicted place in my heart. Coming from a family whose father served honorably and a neighborhood full of others who did likewise, I always had those feelings that I would someday also follow in the same footsteps.

No greater respect do I have for any individual that would put themselves in such danger, physically and mentally, so that others might sleep safely at night.

I will never forget how badly servicemen returning from Vietnam were treated. My older friends were coming back broken and addicted. They were made to feel terrible about the hard sacrifices they made in the war. Today, I am reminded of that treatment every time I see the due respect given to our modern servicemen. Hopefully political winds never sway people back to the disrespectful behaviors of those days.

I often think of how I ran off to the north woods to get far away from all that I saw, and how that option in my life was made possible by our enlisted men and women. I say "Thank you for your service," on a regular basis, but it feels like a weak phrase to describe my much stronger feelings on the matter.

Although I don't take it lightly, I've made peace with how the events of the next chapter shook out.

Chapter 9
Interlude: "A Stitch in Time"

Boston. April, 1968.

When Stan received his draft notice, four years prior to Ringo's rescue shipment, he was living in a Visqueen shack behind the hippy commune at the old "Far Cry" house, and doing LSD every day. Even in his budding hippy days, Stan was trying to get away from the crowds. He had access to a tall, twenty-five room mansion at the commune, yet he chose to build a shack in the woods behind it. The walls were made out of transparent plastic; the frame was comprised of only a few wooden poles. As anyone can imagine, it was pretty cold in the winter. That was when Stan installed his first upright barrel stove. The fire was never allowed to burn at its full potential, though, as there was a major risk of melting Stan's little homeless shelter.

By now, his older friends had already answered their call to war and returned home. Some were okay. Others were not. It is no news that anyone who returned from Vietnam in uniform did not receive a warm welcome. The last time Stan ever saw his old friend Danny was in a bar.

"Stumples." He grinned. It was the closest he came to smiling for the rest of the afternoon.

Danny, like many of Stan's friends, had joined the Air Force. Instead of good "clean" fighting in the bush, they worked nine to five jobs in the cities. The dark, off-hours from five to nine bred boredom, which created a form of unsupervised insanity. For Danny, the memories were too much, and later that evening, Danny cried.

The big oaf that had been Stan's leader and protector for years was reduced to a sobbing junkie, all from his time in Vietnam. He cried to Stan about all of the things he had done in that foreign land, most of which are not fit for this book. Seeing him like that was very sad for Stan, but it also solidified his feelings on the war. He would not be fighting overseas, if he had any say in the matter. It was not the idea of serving the country, but rather the context of the war and the stories he had heard that made up his mind.

At the commune, Stan stared down at his draft notice. He knew then that he had to deal with it. He wasn't interested in fighting in the war, but he also wasn't interested in running from it for the rest of his life. Even though bad news and worse drugs had already made their way back to the states, conscientious objection was not yet an option. Right in that time frame, the only way anyone could avoid being shipped out, other than being physically or mentally unfit, was for religious reasons; but that required actually attending seminary. College already hadn't worked out for Stan, so he knew seminary wasn't on the table either.

He hatched a simple plan: he would go right down to that office and tell it to them straight. The gist of his speech was: "I'm not going to go over there and kill people for you. Just make this simple and put me in jail. I will happily waste my life and do nothing but read books."

He drove his hot rod—he still had a large helping of greaser left in him—down to Local Draft Board 33. It was known for holding the record for the highest number of enlistees in the United States. This record could be attributed to the Boston court's blanket policy. Troubled youth guilty of anything less than murder could be given a clean slate for enlisting in the armed forces. This was the deal that pushed a lot of Stan's friends overseas.

Once he reported to the board, Stan was registered and loaded onto a school bus along with thirty others. The diesel motor rumbled loud, and the draftees were shuffled towards something called "the induction center." While in transit, Stan noticed a particularly vocal man that was repeatedly spouting his condemnation of the war.

Outside of the bus, from the front window to the back, the man hung a huge banner that read "MAKE LOVE NOT WAR." The sign was on display all the way to the induction center. This banner-man took notice of Stan, and offered him a chance to tip the odds in his favor. It was one of many tricks that young men were resorting to during the draft. If they would show high blood pressure, there was a contagious hope that their bodies would be rejected by the military. So, the banner-man offered Stan some speed, which he accepted.

The bus arrived at the induction center. It was a huge building, essentially being used as an assembly line for mass production of soldiers. Inside, people were moved from one room to the next, performing test after test.

The first room looked just like a classroom. Each drafted man and boy sat at a desk one size too small, and filled out forms like students taking a pop quiz. Right away, Stan started messing with his captors. He checked 'yes' for pregnancy and menstrual problems. His eyes were shot and he had every disease in the world. If there had been a box for the black plague, he would have checked it.

Once the "students" turned in their forms, the military officials divided them up into groups. Stan was sent to a bench with seven other people. It only took one look at his bench-mates to realize that he had been thrown in with the troublemakers. The banner-man was right there with him, along with one other conspirator that Stan thought might have actually been crazy. He had a blank stare, did not respond to verbal stimulus, and possessed perfectly nuanced facial twitches. The guy had either lost it, or he had the best act out of everyone on the bench.

Together, the troubled seven and Stan went from room to room. There was the seeing room, the hearing room, and the colonoscopy room. It was a seemingly endless line of examinations. Stan made a game out of every last one of them. Even though he was having fun with the process, he was the only one that didn't have an act. Rather than try to get out for medical reasons, he simply told the truth.

They tested his blood pressure and asked why it was so high.

"Oh, that's because I'm on speed right now," he explained, plain and simple. "I'm not going to kill people for you. Put me in jail." He said this over and over.

For the urine tests, at least two of the others were rubbing their gums until they bled; the theory was that blood in the urine was another way to skip the war. From what Stan understood, that method didn't work. The authorities would keep testing the urine flunkies, sometimes over the course of weeks, watching closer every time. Eventually, all gum-rubbers were caught.

By this point, the troubled seven was down to four. The banner-man and crazy one were still going strong, but some had messed up and accidentally passed a test or two. Others had cracked, and let fly the truth.

Next, the fellowship of insanity was split into separate rooms to see psychologists. If they passed the examination, they would go to war. If they failed, they would have to return and be reevaluated. Like the urine tests, it was a cycle that would be repeated until each subject cracked.

Stan was asked some basic mental evaluation questions. Once again, he answered with the same true story.

"I'm not going to war. Throw me in jail."

He was asked to return in two weeks for another evaluation. The war wasn't off the table for him as far as they were concerned, and neither was jail. Stan had to return to Boston every couple weeks for another psychological evaluation; it went on like this for two months. He knew this was how they eventually wore down their subjects, which gave him an edge. All he had to do was persevere, and remain consistent. He kept up with his standard speech through every visit. His final evaluation was something he would never forget.

The psychiatrist was young, but upper-level in the ranks, a Sergeant Major. He had his own office and a nice desk. Stan took a seat in a fancy, leather upholstered armchair. All of this gave Stan the sense that he had climbed nearly to the top of the crazy ladder. The psychiatrist treated Stan with respect, shook his hand, sat down, and shot the breeze with him for a while.

"Well, we should probably get going on this," he said.

Stan gave his speech.

The psychiatrist looked through his file. Then, he hit Stan with a pop-quiz.

"What does 'A bird in the hand is worth two in the bush' mean?"

Stan had heard the old cliché a thousand times before. Growing up, his mother had been full of these sayings and wisdoms.

"If you have something good," he explained, "don't risk losing it to get something better." It was unclear if this answer was a pass or fail. The next question came.

"What does 'A stitch in time saves nine' mean?"

It was another familiar one. Stan wondered if this was a good or a bad thing. Could this man really send him to war or jail for knowing how to answer these questions?

"If you have a rip in your glove," Stan said, "stitch it right away before the hole gets any bigger."

Silence came, and so concluded the test. The psychologist licked his fingers, and turned a few more pages. He inked his stamp and marked the file with a "*4F Mental*." Stan was labeled as insane; mentally unfit to go to war. It is a status that remains on his military record to this day, though Stan doesn't seem to mind.

He would never be completely certain what made up the doctor's mind, but he developed a theory over time: The psychiatrist had asked Stan the meaning of those old clichés to see if he would put on an act for him, but he didn't. Stan didn't pretend to be crazy or concoct a made-up answer about the moon, the third eye, or his waking visions of angels. He had simply gone right on telling the truth.

It is hard to imagine what course Stan's life might have taken had that doctor not given Stan the diagnosis he needed. It could be said that the evaluation wasn't far off, though, as this wouldn't be the last time that someone called Stan crazy.

Chapter 10

Food for Winter

Tozitna River Valley, Alaska. August, 1973.

Stan stood motionless, his feet parallel, arms at his side. He heard far off birds and all-to-close mosquitos in his ear. His axe stood, handle upright, on the forest floor in front of him. He closed his eyes and imagined the grunting, animalistic charge of a grizzly bear at his back. In one whirling motion he grabbed his axe handle, spun, and buried the axe head right into the skull of the imaginary monster. He was getting faster. Skipper let loose a bark, wondering just what the hell all the commotion was about, and Stan relaxed his grip on axe, letting it slide through his hand back down to the ground.

Bear defense training had become a regular part of Stan's far-reaching hunting and gathering trips for beaver and grayling. His mind was full of "What-ifs," when out alone in the woods. Chiefly among them was, "What if a grizzly bear attacks me while I'm unarmed?" Since landing months ago, he had yet to see one, but he knew they were out there somewhere. Stan practiced the whirling, striking maneuver in rapid succession a few more times before heading home. He would soon discover how utterly hopeless a close range battle with a grizzly bear would really be, axe or no axe.

Returning "home," was a relative term. By now the cabin was only four logs high, and roofless. Finding food for Charlotte, the dogs, and himself was a much bigger priority for Stan. The cabin was constructed only between hunting and fishing forays. Dropping trees and stacking logs hadn't been the only construction project at this point, either. A large pit had already been dug straight down to gravel at the cabin's center. This pit would later be closed off and deemed the root cellar. The water table beneath the pit's bottom continued flowing even through the winter, which kept the entire space at a perfect thirty-two degrees. Essentially, it would be their refrigerator.

The gravel that had been removed from the bush-refrigerator was placed within four trenches, which formed the cabin's foundation. On top of creating a sturdier cabin, this helped prevent the bottom logs from rotting.

Intent on getting the house taller than his dogs, Stan set to work once again that evening.

"UH-kay!" he shouted, and the dogs leapt to their feet, churning up fresh dirt and moss, dragging a large, de-limbed and de-barked spruce tree across the grove. Stan grunted and lifted the log's nose. Charlotte pushed from behind. Without any bark, the tree was made slick with sap, and dragging was easy. Lifting its front half above obstacles, however, was tough to manage for more than ten seconds at a time. Little by little, they dragged the twenty-five-foot log to its destination. This tree would be the next ten inches up for the cabin's southern wall. Once the log was dragged to an exhausted stop, Charlotte returned to one of her preferred activities: gardening. By the summer's end, they would have fresh carrots, potatoes, cabbage and lettuce. It wouldn't last long, but food was at a premium. Thanks to the root cellar, the vegetables would keep fresh, right up until they were eaten.

Of the five hundred pounds of food that Ringo had delivered, some of the weight consisted of heavy cans of juice. To put it simply, Ringo's food run had been critical. It turned the tides of Stan and Charlotte's struggle and kept the dream alive, but it would not carry two people and five dogs through the summer, let alone the winter.

Stan set to work on cutting notches into the log. Since power tools were about as available as Jet Skis, Stan would have to complete the project with only a bow saw, axe, hatchet, and wood planer. Once built, the cabin would not contain a single nail or screw, instead utilizing wooden pegs and in places, simply the force of gravity to hold it together.

Once the log was notched, Stan went to work on producing flat tops and bottoms, so it would sit flush with its upstairs and downstairs neighbors. This required a series of repeated axe attacks along the full length of the log, then numerous passes with a wood planer. The work was, essentially, a blown up version of a boy whittling down a stick with his pocketknife. Once both top and bottom of the log were flat, it was time to lift.

Stan heaved, huffed, and eventually got just the edge of the log onto the south wall. Little by little, he slid the leaning log up to its resting place. With each step of progress that was made, the process grew harder. The walls would only get higher. This process had no tricks with pulleys or straps as one might expect. Stan did not possess superhuman strength either, though he was young and very fit. There was no magic that allowed one young man—with the occasional help from his girlfriend—to lift and set these massive logs, forming them into a home. The process was incredibly slow and grueling.

As in many instances of Stan's life, his personal motto, "perseverance furthers" paid off. Stan would later tell an eager writer, "Some people have no idea what they're capable of doing alone; because they're not willing to try it one inch at a time." This was exactly how the cabin was built, literally one inch at a time.

This is not to say patience and persistence were the only price that needed paying throughout the cabin's construction. Like many young men, Stan was pushing his body to unhealthy limits. He would later recall having back problems in his twenties that most people wouldn't encounter until their seventies.

The cabin had three definitive stages of functionality that needed to be attained. The first priority was to make it bear-proof, then mosquito-proof, and lastly, years later, the roof would be water-proof. Stan repeated the log work over and over; drop, delimb, debark, drag, notch, plane, lift, and set. Following the process from his experience in Canada, Stan stacked the walls towards the sky, two north-south logs, then two east-west logs, and repeat.

Soon it was time to build the gables, the triangular walls at the top of the cabin that would give the peaked roof its shape. This served as somewhat of a relief. Though the lifting continued to get higher, the logs would now be getting shorter. For each gable log, two perpendicular beams, or purlins, were added and securely pegged to keep the high walls from falling in on themselves. Finally, the ridgepole was added to the very peak of the cabin, and the heavy lifting concluded. After that, it was a simple matter (by comparison) of laying countless thin poles, slanting from both low walls, up to the ridgepole at the frame's peak.

On July 1st, 1973, Stan and Charlotte's Tozi River Cabin was complete—mostly.

Stan prepared to make another supply run into town. The snow was long gone, so he would have to rely on packing the dogs, which was fine, considering his sled and snowshoes had burned up in the fire one month prior.

Charlotte stopped him before he could even start packing. She didn't say much, only pointed to the gaping hole in the wall that they had been using as a doorway. Stan had already been planning to leave his .303 British and three dogs for Charlotte's protection while he was away, but understood why anyone might appreciate a strong door, considering the circumstances. He took another three days constructing a door that could have stopped a locomotive. It was made of seven, vertical five-inch logs, each with three spruce poles driven straight through its center, then an additional horizontal top and bottom log to bind them together and seal the deal. Now, the door was complete, the cabin walls were bear proof, and on July 4th, Stan headed to town with Monk and Skipper as trail companions.

Throughout the inbound journey, Stan had time to do some calculations in his head. Between them and the dogs, they had seven mouths to feed. On top of that, Cleetsa was pregnant, and who knew how many pups she would be adding to the mix. It wouldn't be a small number.

On the other side of the equation, they had a small vegetable garden, some flour, and a little remaining beaver meat. There were feeding pools of grayling all up and down the Tozi River, but Stan had nearly fished out anything within reach of the cabin. The same was true with beavers. Every lodge within a five-mile radius had been cleared out of adults. All that remained were the young, for next year's hunting. Stan and Charlotte needed a big animal, preferably an elephant, but a bear or moose would do.

Stan traveled across the Tozi flats, through the valley, up the backside of Fourteen-mile Hill, down, and into the Air Force base known as "The Site." It was another thirty-mile hike, completed in twelve hours. Back in town, an epidemic of excitement had struck. The annual run of salmon had made its way up the Yukon River, like a special delivery all the way from the Pacific Ocean. It was fishing time.

This was no occasion for rod and reel, though. Stan watched in awe as massive wooden fishwheels, like windmills of the river, were pushed out into the current. The current of the Yukon River kept the baskets spinning, which in turn scooped up the upriver bound fish. It was an automatic food producer, though a great deal of work was required in deploying, maintaining, and emptying the device.

Stan wished above all else that they could have such a healthy pulse of fish up where he had built his cabin on the Tozi River, but he had seen nothing of the sort. He assumed the river was too shallow at some point, and briefly considered the logistics of making a prolonged return trip to Tanana in order to gather some Yukon fish of his own, but it simply wouldn't be possible.

He made his usual rounds in town, met a few locals that had heard of his adventures, gathered food, and within twenty-four hours, he was starting his thirty-mile journey towards home.

Close to the cabin, as he crossed the fallen tree that made for a perfect summer-time bridge across the Tozi River, he saw in his peripheral vision something that looked like black spots thrusting their way up the current. Stan stopped, bent down and watched the water with keener eyes. There was a splash, a swift up-river dart, and Stan knew exactly what had happened. A run of salmon had traveled up the Tozi River, and was now splashing its way past their cabin. He ran—no, sprinted into the cabin. Skipper and Monk assumed it was playtime, and started galloping and barking accordingly.

The cabin door flung open and Stan commenced clumsily rooting through the cabin.

"What are you doing?" Charlotte groaned while watching her boyfriend, an agent of chaos, tear through the supplies that she had so recently organized.

Stan barely looked up from the task at hand and told her what he had seen. The idea washed over Charlotte, her eyes widened, and in a flash she was searching through their supplies just as frantically. They grabbed rope, twine, fishing wire, and anything that could be referred to as a strand. Recalling the pattern from his fishing days, Stan started weaving a net. It was a long process, and for four days, Stan had to sit and watch while countless meals swam up river. He was powerless to catch even one.

On that fourth day he cast the net out, and it instantly started to produce. He let out a yelping laugh. They had a new food source, and yet another task to fill their already packed days. Putting up the fish they caught, gutting, cutting, and hanging would be terribly time consuming, but beyond worth it.

Summer crept by and Cleetsa had her litter, a collection of nine pups. The sun had taken to completing nearly full circles in the sky, dipping below the Ray Mountains for only a couple of hours each night before rising for another spin in the blue. At 2 am, the atmosphere was at its darkest, which was still twilight.

Stage two of the cabin, mosquito proofing, had not yet been completed. Per Alaskan summer tradition, the tiny pests were unrelenting, and attacked in clouds. In order to keep from being eaten alive at night, Stan and Charlotte pitched their small, barely two-person tent within the cabin. It was a home within a home.

Stage three, water proofing, was still a far off myth. Stan and Charlotte were able to add a layer of thick Sphagnum Moss to the roof of the cabin, which was capable of absorbing brief showers, but if it poured, the cabin leaked like a sinking submarine. They were still a long way from being able to cover the entire surface with tarp, tin, or anything substantial. What coverage they managed was over only a few key areas, using the inner lining of the dog food bag that had survived the fire. Stan even reallocated his poncho to the roof in the tireless effort to keep the bed dry.

Boyfriend and girlfriend busied their long days putting up salmon after salmon. The run was weak and limited, but it was about a mile better than nothing. They quickly found that the fish were very meager and lean. It was a long swim up to the cabin. Stan compared consuming the fish to eating cardboard, but they seemed to keep the dogs alive. It was a temporary diet that left a lot to be desired. So the majority of the salmon was dried and fed to the dogs. The guts, which couldn't be kept, were consumed right away like a gooey appetizer. This allowed Stan and Charlotte to stretch their dwindling food supply much further than they originally thought they would.

August 1st came, and right on cue, the salmon quit flowing. Stan kept his net in the water for another month to catch the few remaining stragglers. It wasn't much, but every little bit counted. This left a small opening of time in Stan's days, and he turned his focus to trapping. Though his guitar had burned in the fire, one of the thicker strings had survived. He coiled it up and set it within walking distance of the cabin. It was his first snare. He checked it week after week with no results.

He also took to making quick hunting excursions into the woods. Without the snow, the animals were not as easy to track, but he still expected that the supposedly rich river valley would turn up something. Like the guitar string snare, the hunting expeditions yielded nothing. In the end, he found that he didn't need to stray too far from home for food. Many of the big animals would come to him.

It started one afternoon when Skipper perked up, briefly whined, and commenced barking up a monologue. Fifteen minutes later, a chorus of the remaining dog team joined in. Fourteen animal alarms penetrated far into the forest on all sides.

The conclusion of the salmon run had littered the Tozi River banks with countless dead and rotting fish. The smell wasn't too horrendous up at the cabin, but it was enough to attract bears from all over the valley. Before Stan knew what was happening, Skipper took off, racing down to the nearest sand bar. Stan called after him and peered through the trees to find that, despite its size, a grizzly bear had successfully snuck up on them. Stan ran for his rifle while Skipper, to his incredible credit, managed to keep the bear busy. The two animals quickly entangled in combat, Skipper with speed, the bear with power, not to mention a great deal of its own speed.

The grizzly reared up on its hind legs, ready to come down hard on Skipper. Stan took aim with his .303 British Rifle, which he knew to be horribly inaccurate. All the skill in the world couldn't put the bullet where he wanted it. Luck would have to play its hand in the shot. Opening fire would put Skipper at risk, but it was a better alternative to letting the bear win the fight.

He let loose one round and watched it impact directly into the bear's skull. It dropped to all fours, still standing, and made another lunge at Skipper. In that very moment, any hope of conquering a bear with his trusty axe completely abandoned Stan. He fired again, miraculously landing a second headshot, and the bear dropped. Stan released his breath in a sharp puff. He was three years into his twenties, and he had just killed his first grizzly bear.

The conquest aspect of the last thirty seconds was the furthest thing from Stan's mind. Instead, he was thinking of meat. He donned his father's old pair of hip waders, and stepped out into the river. The water sloshed around Stan's legs as he thought through the process to come. The bear's muscle would keep the longest; he would dry it and store it. Its fat was plentiful, and could be used as grease for cooking. Its guts would be quickest to go; he and Charlotte would be eating the liver and heart tonight. Its fur was thick. They would make it into a blanket for the oncoming winter.

That night, Stan cut into the bear's liver and took a bite. Second to the fire that had cost them everything, this mouthful would be his greatest regret of the summer. A horrible sickness struck him. For three days, he slept outside; vomiting instead of sleeping, wondering if his mistake had been fatal.

Charlotte cut into the bear's intestine to find a densely packed, twisting armada of tapeworms. It looked like a severed phone line, packed tight with thin, frayed wires. Though normally, consuming liver was safe and nutritious, this bear had taken one final swat at Stan from beyond the grave. Its diet had been comprised of mostly rotting fish. With no furry food to clean the pipes, the tapeworms grew in abundance. Some were eighteen feet long. Those worms had dumped a plethora of toxins into the bear's bloodstream, all of which ended up in its liver. Stan was very fortunate he hadn't eaten more of it. Though the rest of the bear's muscle was healthy and edible, Stan couldn't bring himself to eat it so soon after The Great Liver Vomiting Incident. Yet again, this was meat that went to the dogs, who seemed to enjoy it a great deal.

August drifted onward and the daylight hours began shrinking by six minutes every day. Stan and Charlotte still had plenty of flour for pancakes every morning, though the bear meat had run its course and the dogs were back to living on dry salmon. Cleetsa's pups were growing rapidly. By now, Stan had installed a narrow window and covered it with two layers of Visqueen in place of glass. It faced out to the river, with a view of the sandbar on which the grizzly bear had stood. Glancing out the window in hopes of seeing something large became a mere reflex for Stan. On an early September day, that reflex paid off, and his eyes caught a large bull moose that had wandered up to the Tozi River bank for some water.

Stan grabbed his rifle and quietly stepped outside. This experience was nearly the exact opposite of the grizzly bear. He had time to think about what he was doing. He watched the towering, silent animal for only a moment, and observed the water trickling from its mouth. He then took his time lining up a good shot, aiming to kill the animal with one bullet. He pulled the trigger, a loud crack awoke the sleeping forest, and the moose fell. It was another first for the young man. The guts went to the dogs, the fat to cooking, and the rest of the meat to plates.

By some other stroke of luck, Stan's guitar string snare also paid off that fall. He arrived one evening to find a lynx caught in the musical strand. It wouldn't provide much more meat than an ordinary house cat might, but like everything else thus far—it was something.

In a flash, October was upon them, and with it came the first light dusting of snow. The temperature was dropping. The sun's schedule had returned to something closer to the Boston rhythm that Stan remembered. It was rising after eight and setting around seven-thirty. Daylight hours would shrink a great deal more before they grew longer again.

These were the circumstances in which the young couple entered the winter: They had a good remainder of moose meat, and three hundred thin salmon for the dogs. There was a dwindling supply of flour and absolutely no firewood prepared. Despite how it may sound, the couple had not enjoyed a single lazy day during the summer. They were simply entangled with the state of being perpetually behind schedule. It was a status that, even with experience, would never let up.

Also as a direct result of the struggle against time, they had not yet managed to replace the snowshoes and sled that they had lost in the fire. Quality winter wear and sleeping bags were nowhere to be seen. Once the deeper snow set in, completing a trip to Tanana would be both difficult and dangerous without these key items. With no way to leave, and no supplies coming in, their condition was uncomfortably comparable to that of the Kellers the previous winter. Above all, with Cleetsa's litter of nine, they now had sixteen mouths to feed. It was a number that would prove to be too high.

Stan building the cabin, one inch at a time.

Skipper, proud king of the hill.

Wearing his father's hip waders, Stan pulls a salmon out of his first homemade net.

Chapter 11
The First Winter

October, 1973

Stan hurtled through the woods, crashing through bushes and leaping over stumps with his rifle in hand. It was already cold enough for the bitter air to sting his throat and chill his lungs as he panted. The raw collection of meat, fat, fur, and guts that was winning the race ahead of him was now more valuable to him than a new car to any suburban dweller. Pursuing grizzlies was another activity that Stan would eventually abandon once he learned how clever, quiet, and swift they could truly be.

The tip of Stan's boot grabbed some extension of Mother Nature's reach. She commanded him to slow down. His speed carried him a good distance forward without the benefit of having feet beneath him. When he finally went down, his right pointer finger was caught between solid earth and the rifle he was holding. The finger's bone fractured. The bear was gone, and considering Stan's newly prone, vulnerable, and injured position, that was probably a good thing.

Most all of Stan's work was done with his hands, and now one of them was half useless. Back home, producing firewood had become a day-to-day process. With the thin winter wear they had, temperatures were already too low for the work to be done outside. So Stan and Charlotte moved two makeshift sawhorses inside the cabin. It wasn't a common job to be seen indoors, but it was their best option at the time. Their stove was far hungrier than any of the dogs. It was the same small tin box that had survived the countless wounds from flying shell casings, making it impossible to shut down. The excessive oxygen supply caused it to burn hotter, and therefore consume wood faster. Despite the stove's condition, Stan and Charlotte had no trouble keeping up with the wood duties, and maintained warmth in the cabin throughout the winter. It was the one thing they had going for them.

The moose meat was incredibly lean. Stan and Charlotte had already lost a great deal of weight, even though they were eating tall, heaping plates of moose for breakfast, lunch, and dinner. The moose simply wasn't filling, unless taken in large quantities. They were already half way through their supply. This was only October.

A trip to town became a necessity, but without snowshoes, a sled, or harnesses for the dogs, they knew it would be a painful, one-way journey. If they were to maintain the way of life they struck out to establish, they needed a way to haul freshly purchased supplies back out to the cabin. If death by starvation came to be close at hand, as a last resort, they were prepared to abandon ship and get to hiking, even though Stan would be wearing moccasins for the entire snow-covered thirty mile journey. If this were to happen, the deep snow, cold, and lack of food would slow them down to a crawl, and they would undoubtedly be stuck spending multiple nights on the trail. The term "night," carried much more heft this time of year. It was sixteen hours long and brought temperatures down to about five degrees Fahrenheit.

Constructing replacement snow gear was slow-going. Stan was doing delicate, difficult crafting work with his right pointer engulfed in useless pain. While he did the construction, Charlotte worked tirelessly to fabricate a harness using the webbing and thread that they had available. She also took to combing excess hair off of the dogs and stuffing it into quilted blankets for warmth at night.

One day, Charlotte stood leaning on the kitchen counter, looking out the Visqueen window.

"How much longer, do you think?" she asked.

Stan told her that at this rate they would be lucky to get going with a functioning sled in three weeks. She looked down at their food supply.

"We have to cut back on flour."

"How much?"

"One tablespoon per day."

She wasn't exaggerating, and starting the next day, rationing began. Charlotte cooked her single daily serving into a small, cookie-sized pancake and nibbled away slowly, savoring the flavor. To Stan, this method involved a meal that was over in a flash and was in no way satisfying. Instead, he took to scooping up a tin full of snow, mixing in the flour, and doing his best to imagine it was a heaping serving of ice cream.

These were the days when Stan's internal motto carried him through. No matter how insane or difficult the task was, if he was losing heart he would only have to repeat two words:

Perseverance furthers.

They went on, scraping forward this way for weeks; cutting firewood, constructing transport, and cooking up a fishy stew for the dogs, all while eating one fourth of a meal per day. Keeping the dogs warm was another constant chore. Stan regularly had to replace their spruce-bough-bedding in order to keep them dry and healthy.

At the very least, Stan and Charlotte had an ample water supply. Parts of the Tozi River remained open and unfrozen throughout the winter, so hydration was one resource they could count on. They hauled the water to the cabin five gallons at a time, up the shallow river bank and thirty feet to the warmth of the cabin.

They were well aware that the rationing would work to keep them going through the grind, but by no means would it power them thirty miles through the snow and cold to The Site. For this, they had a separate stockpile of flour and fish set aside to fuel the final push to town. Pretending the extra food didn't exist was a bigger mind job than anything else during these times. Both Charlotte and Stan felt themselves slowing down. A small cut of moose meat and a tablespoon of flour wasn't enough sustenance.

Another curve ball was thrown when Stan noticed the dogs were losing weight much faster than he had anticipated. It was clear; the planned rations would not be enough to keep the whole team alive. To offset the slim diet, Stan reallocated a full moose quarter to the dogs. This, he would later realize, was another mistake. The meat was extremely lean, and what would have meant another two weeks of food for him and Charlotte disappeared in just two days. Now, the dogs were no better off, and the young couple had lost a significant supply of nutrition. They simply had too many dogs to feed.

There were the original five, full-grown dogs, then nine pups, which were now four months old and rather sizeable. Come travel time, the pups wouldn't be trained to pull a sled; but this didn't change the amount of food they were consuming. Now came the most difficult decision of the winter.

To Stan, dogs were still pets. They were man's best friend, loyal and loving. It was a perception that he would have to emotionally detach from. The situation was edging on inhumane. Stan refused to go on watching the dogs slowly starve to death in the cold. Though they were normally more than able to adapt to the winter conditions, they needed food to do that. They were not only hungry. They were cold. As tough as it was, the math was clear. Fewer dogs in the team would mean more food for the rest.

On November 1st, Stan took one of the younger dogs off leash, and allowed it to run through the snow for a while. This would later become a regular ritual for Stan. For the rest of his life, if a dog was stricken ill or going hungry, he would let it run free for one final day, chasing any smell or whim it desired. After its final burst of freedom, Stan brought the dog out of sight from the rest. His rifle popped, and the moment collapsed into the past.

This was not what he came here to do. Stan had been ready to hunt for food, but not to kill for this. He searched through his options, and reminded himself that what he had done was the lesser of two evils.

The next thought that occurred to the young homesteader was even more troubling, and he almost wished he could forget it. It was a matter of cold logic. There was a shortage of food, and the dog had meat on its bones.

Rather than letting it go to waste, meat from the dog went into a pot, and was boiled into food that would sustain the rest of the team. Then, more cold logic kicked in. The young homesteaders were short on food, too.

Charlotte couldn't bring herself to do what Stan had suggested. Dogs were pets, not dinner. She refused, but Stan accepted it as a necessity. For whichever days he could, Stan would cook and eat the hindquarters of the dogs, and surrender his flour ration, plus any other small game he trapped or killed, to Charlotte. Whatever further food the dog could provide went to the rest of the team. Time went on, days grew darker, cold set in, and with every few days another dog would disappear from the yard.

This was a process that Stan would try to forget, and hoped to never repeat.

Thanksgiving came, and the situation had not improved. Out of nowhere, they received a visitor at the cabin. Enter Russ Wood onto the scene. He and a friend had staked some land of their own on the Tozi River. Wanting to respect unwritten wilderness etiquette, they gave the young couple a healthy distance between their cabins. Both knew that people didn't build cabins on the Tozitna River for the social scene. Russ's future homestead was thirteen miles from Stan and Charlotte. His friend's was eight.

Russ was a genuine outdoorsman, though; and on that Thanksgiving Day, he had decided to take a casual stroll, sixteen miles round-trip, through the snowy neighborhood to see if he could bump into the young Boston couple. With patience and a keen eye, he found the cabin and gave it an unexpected knock.

Russ had not brought any food with him. It was a stroll, not a hike. He had only hoped to say hello and bring a small holiday party favor to the cabin before making his return journey. As the three got to know each other, Russ offered them his gift, a collection of spices for whatever they might be cooking. The young couple popped off the lids of the spices and began eating them handfuls at a time. Russ was likely happy to see his housewarming gift put to such good use.

Stan explained their food shortage. With Russ being who he was, he might have offered them a cut of his own biceps and forearms if he didn't need them for himself. Stan and Charlotte assured him they would make it through. It was looking more and more likely that their trip to Tanana was fast approaching. Stan offered Russ a cut of the only meat they had on hand. Maybe Russ's stance resembled Charlotte's, or perhaps he didn't want to dig into the already non-existent food supply. Whatever his reason, Russ declined. After Thanksgiving, Russ departed and the couple was left to finish the task at hand. They needed to get to Tanana.

On December 15th, Stan and Charlotte consumed extra flour, and the dogs received an extra serving of fish. Finally, the crew struck out on their expedition for town. The sled contained only their tent, sleeping bags, and their remaining, premade pancakes. They crossed the frozen River and headed into the Tozi Flats.

Breaking trail with the sled proved devastating to their progress.

With absolutely no hard pack snow to speak of, they sled was all drag, no glide. They pushed the sled. They pulled the dogs. The Earth's tilt only allowed for three and a half hours of daylight, plus a little twilight on either end. Their first day, they made six of the thirty miles between them and The Site. That night, in their tent, it seemed as though their stomachs had turned upside down from the sudden change in diet. They spent as much time sleeping as they did getting sick. It was negative twenty degrees outside.

They awoke to a thick collection of hoar frost on the tent's walls, formed from their breath. As they climbed out of their sleeping bags, their own body heat melted the frost and turned the tent's interior into a dripping rainforest. Getting wet wasn't just inconvenient and uncomfortable. It was dangerous. The damp conditions caused their parkas and sleeping bags to lose valuable insulation. This night marked the last time that Stan would ever use a tent in the winter. "If you can't heat the tent, don't use it," he would later say. Not only was the melting frost an issue; the time and effort required for setting up and breaking camp simply wasn't worth it. Instead, he would opt to build a fire and sleep close to it. No degree below zero would convince him to do otherwise.

It took another two days and one night's travel before they caught a break. Joe Runyon, the man who had previously been so generous to Stan and given him the bulk of his first dog team, was out running his trapline. He had left the beginnings of a hard pack trail in his wake. Travel became easier, and once they met up with him, he turned around and escorted them back to a survival cabin that marked the halfway point between the Tozi Cabin and The Site. It was a short, ten by ten structure, but it was great in a pinch. There the three spent the night, and enjoyed some dry warmth for a change.

The next day, as the young couple crested 14-mile hill, The Site was indeed, a sight for sore eyes. The trail was hard packed from the sleds and snow machines of Tanana's inhabitants. They soon arrived at the Air Force Base known as The Site, and fell into a tremendous state of relief.

The people working at The Site would welcome Stan and Charlotte back to civilization many times over the coming years, and the homesteaders would one day be delighted to find that a space had been set aside for them to live out of during any visits. It was a small, cramped first aid room. The Taj Mahal of homesteaders.

Each visit, when they arrived, they would do their best to keep the loose down feathers in their mittens from spreading throughout the facility. Between their shedding, wandering in and out, and occasional need to be fed, Stan and Charlotte were often considered The Site's pets.

One of the mechanics let Stan and Charlotte borrow his car for the ten-mile ride down the mountain and into town. They went straight to the general store and bought what food they could. Back up the hill and into their first aid room, the couple found that, in typical fashion, the boys at The Site had pooled any and all surplus food that they had available for a Tozi River relief effort.

The journey back was both easier in some ways and harder in others. The men from The Site loaded a good deal of Stan and Charlotte's cargo onto their snow machines, and helped the couple speed almost a quarter of the way home. This allowed them to make it to Junior's cabin on their first night. From there, the going got tough again. The sled was loaded down with a three hundred pound haul, with only five dogs to pull it. Not far past Junior's cabin, the broken trail was blown over with drift and vanished entirely. Essentially, the sled was plowing through powder rather than sliding across a hard pack surface.

By the time they made it three miles into the Tozi flats, the dogs were in terrible shape. They had simply been surviving on too little food to exert the energy required to pull the load. No muscle to pull. No fat to fuel. Stan and Charlotte had already been snowshoeing alongside the sled and pushing. Now they tried something different. Both strapped into the dog harnesses and became the new team leaders. Side by side, they pulled, along with the dogs, bludgeoning the heavy sled through the snow.

They made it within four miles of the cabin and realized they weren't going to reach it before nightfall. The dogs were beyond exhausted, Stan and Charlotte had been sweating and soaking through their clothes. The entire population of the Tozi River valley—Stan and Charlotte—had seen a dramatic decrease of public interest in camping over the past week. It looked like they were in for another night tucked in sleeping bags without a fire in weather that had now dipped to forty below zero. Then they realized they had another option. At the risk of losing a portion of their new food supply to the various critters of the Tozi flats, Stan and Charlotte abandoned their entire load and made a run for the cabin. It felt like a race compared to the previous miles, and they arrived to the safe and soon-to-be warm the cabin just after sundown.

Morning came and Stan took the dogs out for another spin. He loaded up the food, which was right where he left it and thankfully had not been ripped open. Before leaving the open flats, he pulled one new item out of the snow, and threw it onto his sled. Months earlier, Stan had seen an empty and abandoned fifty-five gallon oil drum on the flats. He already knew how to convert it into a stove, and now was the time to do it. The barrel would yield a larger firebox as well as better control of oxygen flow, and therefore a manageable rate of burn.

It's difficult to refer to the remainder of that winter as easy, but by comparison to early days, it truly was. Rather than spending all day constructing new transportation, Stan was able to use the sled to run his trapline, which would eventually become a healthy source of the low income that was needed for life on the Tozi. That first year Stan and Charlotte didn't sell many pelts, as they had their own uses for the fur. By the winter's end, Stan had one beaver and one marten pelt remaining for sale. He took them to town, and made the first portion of his annual salary: fifty-two dollars.

While out running his trapline and hoping for some smaller catches, Stan stumbled across something much bigger. There was a bull moose standing about twenty-five yards off the trail. Moments like this would later become a practiced art of precision and grace. Stan would call for the dogs to stop, knowing that he had exactly five seconds between calling "Whoa!" while the dogs were looking back at him before they yanked the sled with full force to chase after the animal, thus ruining Stan's shot. Before even stopping, Stan would have his gun out of its scabbard; ideally he would even manage to cock it. Just after stopping the sled, at the one-second mark, Stan would press his snow hook down, which is an essential braking mechanism in dog mushing used to keep the dogs running off with the sled. At about the four-second mark, he would rest his rifle on the bars, thus improving accuracy tenfold, and take his shot just before the dogs made a single sound.

This first sled-to-moose encounter, however, went nothing like that.

Stan didn't have a snow hook, or know what one was for that matter. He called, "Whoa!" and knocked the sled to its side, hoping that the increased drag would at least slow the dogs down if they decided to go for a jog. At about the eight-second mark, the dogs were having a party, yanking on the sled, and the moose went to alert status. Stan let loose the best shot he could under the circumstances, and the moose collapsed. Although it was only late February, this meat meant a healthier remainder of winter, and marked the definitive end of the famine that had plagued them throughout their first days in the cold.

The birchwood trapping sled that Stan constructed despite his broken finger, during his first winter on the Tozi.

<u>Stan</u>
On Hunting, Trapping, and Everything Else

There's a sign that's been hanging above my door for a while now. It's a very simple African hunting chant that I once came across:

"Be patient, be careful, try again, and again, and again."

Chapter 12
Loners and Innovations

March, 1974.

The sled glided to a stop right in front of the cabin. Stan stepped off into what little snow remained of the season. This would definitely be his last trip to town until fall came back around and the fluffy white flakes started piling up again. The sled was loaded up with a collection of supplies. The dogs had moved their legs just about all they cared to for the day. One by one, Stan returned each yelping furball to its chain and box. That was when he noticed a few missing items.

Each dog normally had a bone to gnaw on. All of them were gone. On top of that, the bowls used at mealtime were also missing. Stan opened the cabin door and asked Charlotte if she had seen or heard anything. She hadn't. They had a thief on their hands, and quickly began narrowing down suspects. Marten were too small, beavers were disinterested, and bears were too loud.

Out in the woods, Stan and Charlotte found each of the bowls licked shiny. They returned what they could find to its rightful place, and that night, they waited. The sun was on its way to bed when the dogs sounded their customary alarm. Stan and Charlotte stepped outside to find the perpetrator. On the edge of light, nearly motionless, the eyes of a black wolf were peering back at them. Fortunately, they were not dealing with a full pack. Most packs spent their days roaming the Ray Mountains and Tozi Flats, happily hunting and feasting on caribou. Often times, Stan and Charlotte would sit outside and listen to the distant howls of far off packs without a single worry.

This was different, though. It was a lone wolf, cleaved from the pack either for age, stamina, or a shake up in the command structure. It was hungry, which made it desperate. Killing the wolf wouldn't have made for much meat, and the fur was in bad shape. Domesticating the animal was out of the question, so feeding it would simply be taking food from the dog's mouths and encouraging the predator to return. Stan hollered at the ragged creature, fired one shot up into the air, and it vanished into the shadows. It would not be the last time that those quiet eyes watched the cabin, waiting for a chance to catch a meal.

A second night, a third night, and a fourth, the wolf returned. Stan took aim on the fifth night, and brought the wolf's life to an end. He approached the carcass and saw that it was far more famished than he could have imagined. Enclosing both hands around the wolf's waist, Stan could not only touch thumbs and pointer fingers together, he could bring them past each other. The wolf was skinnier than he had ever seen his sled dogs.

In the past, his inner hippy quietly spoke up when he killed a moose, trapped a marten, or drove the dogs hard into the wind. The voice was a whisper—as killing was a necessity and he wasn't about to stop—but it was there; telling him that all of it seemed too brutal. Now, the voice would get even quieter. In the wolf's famished body, Stan saw that he was not responsible for bringing brutality to the Tozitna River valley.

Nature itself was brutal.

The young couple couldn't have known at the time, but encounters identical to this one would become an almost regular occurrence each spring, especially after a long, difficult winter. Sometimes they would succeed in scaring the wolves off. Most times they didn't. What little meat those wolves provided went into the dog pot, and poured into the previously stolen bowls of the team.

There were other visits, though, that were significantly less mild. One spring day, a dark haired wolf stepped out onto the still frozen Tozi river ice. Skipper, still secure in his title of leader of the pack, was now tasked with defending the rest of the team. He was the only one off leash.

Without hesitation, he dashed out onto the ice to meet the wolf head on. They circled each other, snarling and never breaking eye contact. It was not an even match, not by a longshot. This wolf was healthy, and strong. It had honed its skills to kill in one bite, and been forced to fight other dogs all of its life. Skipper was smaller and only got into fights twice a year at most, always with smaller sled dogs. He was a fighter, but the wolf was a professional killer.

The wolf of the wild and the half wolf of the team continued to circle each other for another tense fifteen seconds. To Stan's surprise, when the game was done, the wolf tucked its tail between its legs and cautiously made his retreat. Apparently, Skipper's years of winning fights against smaller dogs had given him a skewed, yet strong sense of confidence. It fooled the wolf.

Victorious, Skipper stood out on the river ice with a freshly inflated ego, and no idea how close to death he had come.

The next two years were a time of tremendous innovation. Really, every year that Stan and Charlotte spent on the Tozi could be defined as such, but these first two brought their homestead from a functioning shelter to a place they could call home.

Stan took to burying fertilized salmon eggs in the river's gravel in the hopes of increasing the size of the run. This was a concept Stan had known of even before being dropped off by the nervous pilot in 1973. Since it would take four years before the life cycle brought the increased numbers, Stan had made his first efforts at salmon spawning soon after the cabin's construction during their first summer, using only a shovel and his hands to deposit the eggs. The second summer, he utilized a metal funnel to insert the eventual fish deeper into the ground. By the third year, he had used PVC piping to construct a giant syringe, which could be used to inject the future dog food deep into the riverbed.

Stan studied the fish. He was intent on replenishing what he removed, as well as establishing secure and healthy runs. It would be remiss not to say that he also wondered just how much he could manipulate nature. He made a regular habit of donning a pair of goggles, slipping into the crystal clear waters of the Tozi, and observing the fish's reproductive method. He saw females swimming along and dropping unfertilized eggs on the riverbed. Next, he watched as males deposited milky sperm to the eggs below. He read endless literature on the salmon and learned of the critical phase that eggs entered twelve hours after fertilization, in which so much as a splash could bring the process to a fatal halt. He even went as far as having numerous egg jars within the cabin, testing minor tweaks in his operation in order to perfect it. It was as though he could, at will, transform between homesteader and mad scientist.

Before summer seasons, as long as there was snow, Stan feverishly made trips to and from town, gathering metal, junkyard machinery, and anything he foresaw being able to use for construction or homemaking. On one trip to town, he purchased enough string and line to craft an entirely new fish net, increasing his range from twenty to fifty feet. This, along with other breakthroughs, brought the couple's salmon count from three hundred to one thousand by the end of the second year.

Stan used scraps of corrugated tin, oil barrels, and hardware collected from town to construct numerous farming implements. One such project involved crafting various metals into a makeshift plow. After breaking up the earth with a shovel, Stan could harness the dogs to the plow much like he would a horse or mule, call "Okay!" and churn up one fifty-foot row after another for a new and improved vegetable garden. The gardening and farming operation would continue to expand at an impressive rate, year by year.

Eventually, Stan annexed an entire island on the Tozi River for the sole purpose of gardening. Its place in the middle of the river allowed for ample sunlight and terrific irrigation. He cleared what smaller trees were there and began breaking up the ground. Then he gathered yet another fifty-five gallon oil drum, painted it black to absorb as much heat as possible, and composted the remains of any fish he caught. On a hot day the barrel would produce up to five gallons of pure liquid fish fertilizer. Every year, by the summer's end, the barrel would be completely empty. The organic material would have been completely broken down, bones and all. Only the smell remained.

Using an angle iron, a pole, and the molding heat of fire, Stan crafted his very own scythe. The grass he harvested with this implement would turn into much valued hay and keep the dogs warm throughout the winter. Next, he constructed a larger, higher, sturdier food cache in order to keep their nourishment out of reach from the bears.

As time continued its tumble, Stan managed to drop moose and bear in increasing numbers on the sandbar that he could see from inside the cabin. Depending on the time of year, though, he would have to let some of the animals go. The river current between him and the meat was too strong and too deep. Even if he found his way across the river, there would be no way to transport the meat other than dragging it up river. Stan's mental shipyard immediately commenced designing the first in a long line of boats that would forever be classified, "cool breezes."

With schematics racing through his mind, Stan laid out a framework that was both efficient and easy to construct. It was essentially a long log with an outrigger. Stan ripped the bark off of a former tree and took a planer to all the knots and branches for improved hydrodynamics. He flattened the top and nailed down boards in two places; one for a seat, one for cargo. To keep the cool breeze from rolling and dumping both Stan and the dinner, he constructed a crude outrigger using three poles.

If "cool breezes" could be considered bush canoes, the next vessel to leave Stan's shipyard would be a battleship by comparison. At this time, though, its design had yet to be conceived, and its construction would not commence for another eight years. It would also be a few years until Stan was gifted a proper canoe with a five horsepower motor. Until then, "cool breezes" were the only mode of water transportation he had.

They were a surprisingly successful design, and managed to keep Stan's pants dry, even with a moose quarter loaded onto the cargo bay. Often times, Stan would walk along the river bank, line his "cool breeze" five miles upriver, and enjoy a peaceful float down, which made for excellent, quiet hunting along the riverbank.

A few other cabins sprouted up on the Lower Tozi, where the water was deeper and easier to travel by boat. Eight miles down sat Jack Bloom and his wife Karen. Jack was gregarious, laid back, and enjoyed nothing more than sitting down with a cup of coffee and conversing about everything under the sun. Karen, on the other hand, possessed immense energy, and a sharp, quick memory that outmatched everyone on the Tozitna River. She was known for remembering important dates in other people's lives that they themselves had long since forgotten. Anniversaries and birthdays rested safe and sound in Karen's mind. She was an encyclopedia without making an effort.

On one occasion, in passing, Jack asked Stan exactly how old he was. Stan started counting, and Karen answered for him.

Another mile and a half down river from Jack and Karen sat Tom Fogg. He was a young bachelor who had returned from his tour of duty in Vietnam as a Green Beret. When military jets broke the sound barrier over the Tozi River valley, as was common in those days, Tom's reflexes would make him hit the deck the very moment the sonic boom rattled the forest. He was gifted in the art of conserving valuable supplies like food and fuel, and maintained a healthy cache of end-times gear and supplies, just in case the rest of the world took a turn for the worse. It wasn't an incredibly outlandish precaution, as evidenced by the supersonic training maneuvers above. The Cold War was standing on everyone's doorstep.

Another two miles down river, there was Bill and Marie Fliris. The best woodworking and crafting came out of Bill's cabin. He had a visual mind. Whereas Stan never completely finished a project past functionality in his life, Bill took time to varnish, detail and dress his sled. Everything he constructed was a work of art, whereas everything Stan collected was an accumulation of junkyard rejects and rough cut wood, but they all worked great.

For the second winter go-around, it was Bill Flires that loaned Stan a small, one handed chainsaw. To this day, if Stan were forced to choose only one piece of modern equipment for use in the wilderness, it would be a chainsaw. The tremendous time and effort it saved, despite it being incredibly small and low powered, was invaluable.

Bill's wife, Maria, was a starry eyed young woman that was far more acclimated to city life than the homesteader existence. She was content just the same, though, as she was there to be close with Bill, not the bears and moose.

Lastly, another two miles down river sat Russ and Anne Wood, at the end of the line. Russ had grown up the son of a Fairbanks potato farmer, and therefore had the work ethic of two men. He wore glasses, which he always pulled down his nose to cast surly looks to his neighbors. What Russ suffered from most was a case of chronic generosity. He was insistent on helping anyone he could, and persistent in denying any assistance in return.

If by chance, someone were able to slip a favor through Russ's defenses, he would be sure to return it twofold. His almost non-existent temper had record cool-down speeds, and after a frustrating incident, Russ would return to his normal relaxed state within minutes. His wife,

Anne, had some incredible source of strength from deep within that she often drew from. She was consistently seen working side by side with Russ no matter what the task, from hauling wood to construction.

So sat the Tozi bunch; secluded, yet not alone. Jack the gregarious, Karen the quick, Tom the survivor, Bill the craftsman, Maria the city girl, Russ the generous, and Anne the workaholic. They all grew to be close friends, though socializing wasn't a regular part of life. This was especially true in the summer, when the river water was low and the snow had melted from the trails. Of all the federal land in Alaska that had opened up in the seventies, the Tozitna River Valley had been one of the furthest plots from civilization. It was no coincidence that these nine would end up in sharing the same river. They were adventurers, lovers of nature, and knew where to find their own kind.

At Stan's homestead, the dogs ran free all day. They would split off into the woods, out of sight to chase critters, eat fish right out of the water, and wag their tails in peace. Consistently, at each day's end, the dogs returned home for one final, home cooked meal. Stan found their breath to be absolutely atrocious. From their wolf lineage, dogs were better suited to eat partially decomposed food, including rotten fish. For Stan, each evening became a desperate struggle to keep the dogs from giving him a few love-licks to the face while he fed them.

Stan's traplines expanded and their efficiency improved. Better trapping meant more money, and more money meant better traps. Charlotte ran a trapline of her own. She spent a tremendous amount of time pressing her foot into a treadle, sewing pants, fur hats, and mitts. She weaved baskets and made beautiful floral and butterfly collages, compressed behind glass and set in a frame. The proceeds from all of this work went directly to anything needed in the winter that couldn't be grown, hunted, or scavenged.

The couple was by no means rich, but they didn't have to be. Between traplines and crafting, they survived on a combined annual income of two thousand dollars, or less. Stan often joked of these days as the time they started "coasting." It's a horribly inaccurate term; but within Stan's realm of existence, coasting only required non-stop, tireless work. As long as their lifestyle wasn't on the starving brink of collapse, life was considered easy.

*One of many improvements at the homestead; a new bear cache (left,)
next to the old one, (right.)*

Stan and Charlotte out for a ride in a "cool breeze."

The homestead expands, as an old smokehouse is converted into a storage shed and deemed "Stan's Place."

<u>Stan</u>

On the Cold

I'm not sure if it would be right have a book about my life without paying tribute to the cold. Each year, after the first three days of deep freeze, you get used to it as much as you ever will. More than bears, fire, and starvation: the cold is the one that kills. It's just not the painful, brutal killer that many would to expect.

Once, I was on mile seventeen of a twenty-mile snowshoe trip across deep snow when I took a break that I shouldn't have. I was young, and my winter clothes were still a work in progress—not very warm. I also had a slight fever at the time. All of a sudden, an incredible warmth washed over me. Soon after the physical feeling, my mind relaxed into a state of peace. It was a trap. I was rapidly falling into a death sleep, and completely willing to accept it.

From somewhere deep in my memory, I suddenly recalled what this feeling really meant. I couldn't tell you who it was, but someone had warned me about this exact calming sensation. That conversation, which probably happened years prior, saved my life. Little by little, I tried scaring myself. I created this… self-inflicted sort of freak-out. It wasn't about motivation that time, not at first. I had to hit myself with fear. The determination came next. I knew that stopping again would end me.

It's important to take everything in stride, and roll with the punches, but not with cold. From that day forward, I knew what to look for, and kept on my toes.

Chapter 13

Spooked

Winter, 1975

January was no time to be messing around; he knew this. Sure, he was only twenty-five years old, and maybe some of his hardest lessons lay still ahead. It didn't matter; this was already his second winter in Alaska. He knew it got cold. He knew it got dark. Above all, he knew there was no such thing as a plan, but instead, an ever-devolving state of affairs that hopefully concluded with him breaking even, filling his stomach, and warming by the fire at the day's end. Once this particular ride concluded, Stan Zuray would have none of these things.

On that frozen day, Stan harnessed his dogs to the sled before dawn. It wasn't hard; the sun itself wouldn't be climbing out of bed until about eleven or so. Once it did, Stan hoped to cover as many miles as possible with that warmth and visibility on his side. The goal was to make it halfway home, to Junior's cabin, in time to cook and eat some of the very food he was hauling.

This was not to say that Stan was picky over whether his food was hot or cold, wet or dry. In fact, he had recently become very accepting of what he referred to as "trail food" and what others called "commercial dog feed." The dry pellets were full of nutrition, required no preparation, and could be eaten one handful at a time while riding the dog sled, fresh from the pocket of his own parka. The locals, and anyone Stan met for that matter, had a good many laughs over this, and Stan often laughed with them. Like everything else in Stan's world, form followed far, far behind function.

Leaving from The Site rather than town, as he always did, brought his journey from forty miles down to thirty-three. Junior's Cabin, the halfway point between there and home, lay sixteen miles away. It would have been nothing if not for the heavy supply load, which in turn would have been impossible if not for the dogs.

Stan removed his hook from the hard pack snow of The Site.

"UH-kay, UH-kay!"

With that command, Stan's five dogs started pulling, and he started kicking. The new, heavy freight sled glided forward, away from the light, heat and comfort of the base, into the dark and cold of the thin spruce forest through which the trail cut. It was thirty below zero when Stan got underway.

Once his momentum was strong, Stan was free to think, plan, and let his mind wander, as he so often did on those long hauls between the Tozi and Tanana. He did the math on how much longer the dogs, he, and his wife might make it with a food haul like this. He listened to the dogs panting; he watched their little paws work, checking for signs of pain, struggle, or injury. If they came to a steep uphill, Stan got off and pushed.

Thanks to heavier snow machine traffic out of Tanana from hunters and trappers, the trail was well established. The sled was able to skate on top of the hard-pack, and the dogs had no issue following the line, even in the dark.

Stan and his team slowly climbed 14-mile hill just as the sun was cresting the horizon. It was shaping up to be one of those days, the rare ones where the state of affairs didn't deteriorate, but mended. The dogs were making great time, and the sun had a way of breathing confidence into a man.

They topped the hill. Though it was far from the last obstacle between Stan and home, it was at least the last major climb he and the dogs would be dealing with. Right at that point, Stan got his first glimpse of the trouble that lay ahead. In other circumstances, it might have been beautiful.

A soft ice fog had rolled in. This, combined with a ten mile an hour wind that was kicking up powder and whirling it from here to there, had created complete white out conditions. So much for visibility.

"Uh-kay, Uh kay!"

The dogs pressed on. The hard pack of the popular hunting trail quickly dispersed in the wide-open land on the backside of 14-mile hill.

What trail remained was blown over by snowdrift from the growing wind. This alone was not a fatal blow, as there were still trail markers every hundred or two hundred feet.

The downward slope of the trail increased slightly faster than Stan recalled in the past. Soon, the sight of unfamiliar, thin spruce trees told Stan he was not where he meant to be at all. They had gone off trail, and he couldn't be sure how long ago it had happened.

"Whoa! Whoa!"

Stan slammed the brake down into what he now felt was mostly powder. There was some crust, but definitely not enough to constitute a trail. The dogs stopped. Some looked back at Stan with curious eyes, yelping and panting, perhaps wondering why he forced them to break such incredible pace. Meanwhile, Stan, unsure of exactly how much time they had lost and how far off the trail he was, trudged through the snow to the front of the team and grabbed hold of Cleetsa, his lead dog. Slowly, he turned the team around, faced them back up the hill from which they had descended, and started pulling back upwards with them. His new, heavy, and fully loaded freight sled made this a difficult task.

One hour, and one unplanned climb later, the team was back on the trail.

"UH-kay! UH-Kay!" Stan panted.

Away they went. Before long the downward slant increased, and Stan found himself once again standing amidst uncharted trees. This second incident spelled great concern. It didn't make much sense. This team, with Cleetsa at the lead, had driven this same trail twenty times before. Heavy snow and drift hadn't stopped them in the past. So why, when north meant home, was Cleetsa insisting on taking them east?

Again he turned the team around, and again he helped them climb yet another unplanned hill. It wasn't the loss of time and sunlight that concerned Stan the most. By this point, both excursions through deep powder had cost him valuable energy. Worse yet: he had been sweating excessively. To be cold and tired was simply traveling, but to be damp was a whole other, more dangerous story.

As he hiked uphill, back onto the trail a second time, the cause of the problem hit him, literally, in the face.

The wind.

He turned back to see Cleetsa, shying and pawing away from the harsh blow. It was blustering, not incredibly fast, but very consistently from the West. The realization was both obvious and extremely troubling. Here he was, halfway into his journey, three quarters of the way through his sunlight, damp with sweat, and dragging around a lead dog that preferred to go where the wind took her. It was a miserable time for the canine to start up her sailing career.

There wasn't much he could do. He needed Cleetsa. The other dogs in the team were good ones to be sure, but none of them were leaders. Even Skipper, a dog with half wolf blood, though large and strong, had not yet lead a team on this trail. Stan would try again, only this time, knowing what to look for. He would catch Cleetsa in the act before she dragged them too far off course. If they could just get out of the wind, maybe she would find her loyalty again from somewhere deep within, and remember that it was Stan who fed her, not the breeze.

Again and again she veered to the east. Again, and again, Stan stopped the team and put them back on course. It was no good. The time and energy lost at this rate would mean finding the cabin long after nightfall, if at all. Against his better judgment, Stan unclipped Cleetsa from the team entirely. It would later be his greatest regret in a day that was full of them. He called out, the remainder of the team started pulling, but the problems didn't stop.

"Get outa there!" Stan yelled into the wind, but Cleetsa had long since blocked out his commands. Now free to roam, once Stan and his team had gotten moving, Cleetsa's new habit was to run out to the front of the team, reassert herself as their leader, and gradually lead them all eastward towards freezing and or starving to death. Worse, the dog was already scared of Stan from past punishments on the trip. With Stan so tired, and Cleetsa so light, catching and harnessing her to the rear of the team as a wheel dog was a simple impossibility.

Stan was now at war. He didn't think the dog was trying to kill him. Hell if he knew what she might have been thinking. Now that he was forced to confront her, he realized that she had been growing a little spooky over the past year. Once, she had nearly lead Stan and his team clean off a cliff and into a pile of their own broken bones, sled, and spirits. Maybe she was some kind of maniacal crazy, or maybe she just didn't like the cold.

Stan armed himself. The Gi pole tied to the side of his sled was about six feet in length. Normally, it was used to steady the sled on uneven terrain while the driver walked in front. Stan had different intentions.

"Uhhh-kaayyy..." He panted, and the race was on. In the snow behind them, Cleetsa perked up and gave chase. Stan turned and watched the least loyal dog he had ever owned make her speedy approach. Unrestricted by the burden of the load, Cleetsa was faster than Stan and his team could ever be.

The remainder of the team panted away, sticking to the trail. If Stan could keep Cleetsa behind them, he had a shot at making the cabin. Between Stan's arm and the gi pole it carried, he had about an eight-foot defensive radius. Now, riding half backwards on the sled, Stan took his first swing at Cleetsa. She dodged it.

Another swing, and Cleetsa dropped back. The plan was far from perfect. Stan was wildly using energy and breaking sweat by swinging a six-foot pole, all while facing the wrong direction on a sled being driven by a team without a leader. This was certainly improvising. He saw now that he was in for the standard, ever-devolving state of affairs after all.

In one pass, Cleetsa swung wide, out of Stan's reach. The deep powder off the trail served to slow her down and the odds of the race were balanced out.

"Get up there! Get up there!" Stan called, and the tired remains of his team pulled harder still. The classic neck-and-neck status was maintained for only a short time. Cleetsa found her way, pouncing through snow almost as deep as her ears, and once again ran out in front of the team. She brought them all off the trail, to the east.

Stan was beat. The sun was so low in the sky he could touch it. He rustled through his pack and pulled out a jar of peanut butter. It was beyond frozen. The temperature had climbed to negative twenty during the day, but once the sun went down, it would be back to the negative thirties. After that, he would have to traverse the valley ahead, which always brought an additional ten degrees of cold.

Still hot from hate and pole-swinging adrenaline, Stan chipped away at the peanut ice, considering everything: his sweat-soaked under layers, the setting sun, and the possible forty-below ride through the valley he was facing. Stan's nerve endings had already gotten tougher for the winter, or suffered damage depending on how you looked at it. That didn't mean his thick skin would protect him from freezing, not tonight. He ate, hoping the fat content would give him that extra shred of warmth and energy that he so desperately needed. He eyed the rebel dog while crunching away at the tasty ice.

"You're going to get us killed."

Cleetsa, seeming to know exactly whom Stan was talking to, looked up from her important sniffing business in the snow. A flicker of obedience almost made Stan feel as though he could order her to roll over and play dead, though this was far from the case.

"Home is that way." Stan pointed north. "What's that way?" He pointed east.

Cleetsa barked, in so doing she started the whole team barking.

"SHUT UP!"

Silence again. At the very least, Stan had enough authority over the rest of the team to keep them quiet.

He couldn't believe it had come to this, but the situation was becoming undeniable. It was Cleetsa, or Stan and the rest of his team. He eyed Cleetsa one last time, then made his decision. He was mad, even enraged with the dog, there was no denying that; but no amount of anger had, or would ever cause Stan to wish suffering on one of his dogs. A firm blow to her head would at least be quick and painless.

As she drew closer to the team, Stan made sure to make no sudden movements. The dog was spooked, but she had to be hungry.

One more step.

Cleetsa stayed at a safe distance for what seemed like three sunsets. Finally she took two more steps in and—

Stan swung the pole with everything he had left. Cleetsa jumped, turned and ran, but not fast enough. The pole crashed into her hind leg, dealing a brutal compound fracture. She yelped and twisted, snapping her jaws at an attacker that was no longer there.

The last Stan saw of Cleetsa that day, she was running on three legs, off into the white out, her back right leg flailing wildly behind her. He had aimed to knock her out, and instead doomed her to a slow, cold death somewhere on 14-mile hill. Stan lowered his head, both in exhaustion and frustration that the situation had escalated to this point. He pounded a fist on his sled, now angrier at himself than he ever had been at the troubled dog.

Into the valley he went. The sun dropped, as did the temperature. The cold was so terrible, in fact, that Stan found himself doing something he never thought he would. He pulled his hat over his face, obscuring most of his vision, except for the few shreds of light that made it through the fibers of his cap; he had to trust Skipper to do the navigating. At one point, Stan realized that Skipper wasn't following the hard-pack trail that the team had traveled before. He had instead found a deeply ingrained rut in the ground that ran roughly parallel to Stan's normal pathway. This was the old Allakaket trail, which had existed long before pioneers made contact with Athabascan natives. As the sled careened down the aged trail, Stan wondered if perhaps it was Skipper's inherited tracking instinct, passed down from his wild lineage, that was saving both of their lives.

The remaining miles went by in a painful, cold blur. Skipper held true, and the cabin was found. Stan stumbled off of the sled, not bothering to secure the dogs, and plowed into the cabin. It was a small plywood shack, not meant for much more than survival. Stan collapsed on the floor and curled into a ball, completely skipping any effort to make a fire. Exhaustion and freeze made terrible allies.

He was shivering in darkness. Then:

RIIIIPPPP.

Stan awoke to the sound. He was in a cold—but thankfully still alive—daze.

RIIIPPP.

Rushing and tumbling, he worked his way to the door and threw it open. There stood Skipper, still harnessed to the sled, but now standing on top of it. He was aggressively tearing into the dog feed that they had all worked so hard to carry this far. Stan felt a fierce disciplinary yell reflexively rise in his throat. Then, he stopped it. He watched the feasting dog that had, above all odds, saved his life.

"Go ahead, I guess you earned it."

If Skipper could speak, he probably wouldn't have said thanks.

Stan went back into the cabin and, having regained dexterity in his fingers, started a fire. He thought of Cleetsa, where she might be, and what could possibly have caused a dog to completely lose it like she had. He thought by now, she must have succumbed to the cold and the snow. Freezing to death typically began with bitter pain, which progressed to a warm numbness, then nothing. Hopefully she had passed calmly from pain, to sleep, to death.

Cleetsa was found seven miles away, and one day later. Though Stan wasn't there to witness the discovery, one can imagine it went something like this:

"Hey man, come look at this!" shouts the cook. He had been freshly transferred to The Site only one week prior, and is now looking at his first taste of how truly brutal life up here could be.

"Jesus. She's one of Stan's."

"What the hell happened to her leg? Come here, girl."

Cleetsa takes a tentative step closer to the cook.

"What kinda man lets this happen to a dog? He just left her to die?"

The tender cook feeds her some table scraps, and from that moment on, he and the dog are forever bonded.

"We're gonna fix you up with some nice digs, pup. How do you like steak?"

Stan later discovered that Cleetsa had been rescued. Although their relationship was strained, Stan was relieved and only wanted the best for her now. Her leg mended, she would go on to live happily in her military-grade, heated dog box. While she ate steak for the rest of her years, Stan went right on riding the same snowy trail, occasionally downing a handful of commercial dog feed to keep himself going.

<u>Stan</u>
On Dogs and Cleetsa

George Attla says, "A dog can do no wrong," and I've always agreed with that. They get just about all of their bad habits from humans. Most of that human conditioning, whether or not it was intentional, is tough to un-train. I'm not sure what Cleetsa had been through, but before running in my team, and before Joe Runyon's team, a human had completely killed her sense of loyalty.

Lucky dog, it all worked out for her in the end.

Stan's "show off" photo. His new 300 Winchester Magnum in one hand, and one of Skipper's pups in the other. His new chainsaw, and his lead dog at the time, Arnie. The fur of a large black bear towers behind him.

Chapter 14

Grizzly

Fall, 1975.

Stan and Charlotte stalked along the Tozi River with speechless lips and searching eyes. They gripped the chains tightly. Between the two of them, they were holding back a total of three eager dogs. It was autumn now, a sweet spot for hunting. The outcome of this hike would likely determine if they would be losing weight, or keeping it this winter. Before the humans in the pack saw anything, as usual, the dogs caught a scent and started barking. Stan and Charlotte dropped low, shushing the dogs and whacking them with a willow branch to keep them quiet. Down the trail ahead of them was their prey, a three hundred pound grizzly bear.

They crept closer, hoping the dogs wouldn't play their hand too early and alert the bear. Both homesteaders had rifles now; Stan with his .303 British, and Charlotte with a Winchester Model 70 .338 magnum. The new rifle had been gifted to them by yet another generous Tanana resident. As they approached firing range, boyfriend and girlfriend cast a look to each other, saying "ready," without speaking. All at once, the dogs were set free, and a scrambling, clinking canine stampede commenced.

It was the strangest thing. Outside of the cabin, there were times that Stan saw the dogs peacefully co-existing with grizzly bears and drinking out of the same river. Yet once they were confined to chains, the temperament shifted gears, from neutral to drive.

The dogs reached the bear and entangled him in a flurry of swats, jumps, and snaps. It was a maneuver inspired by Skipper's first tussle with the species. Stan and Charlotte stood in unison and took their firing positions.

From the days of shooting out Boston street lights with zip guns, Stan's aim had steadily improved. When a Tanana local named John Hewitt visited, Stan's marksmanship reached full potential. John taught Stan to breathe, aim, and control where the bullet went. He was a true marksman. Prior to, Stan managed roughly a three-inch grouping at one hundred yards. John brought it down to an inch and a half.

For each shot taken on that training day, Stan would bend down, pick up the shell casing, and pocket it. Perhaps the ecological consideration of keeping the valley litter-free played somewhat in this act; but mostly, it was another way to stretch the US dollar. Stan reloaded every bullet casing he fired.

Now, he would be placing a .303 caliber bullet in a tangled mix of friendlies and adversary. Stan fired high, hoping to take the bear down in one shot. He didn't. Charlotte followed up with a wider, more powerful bullet, and the bear made its slow collapse. It might sound like a Hollywood edit, but after years of using this method, not a single dog was killed or injured in the process.

The pair had been out in the woods long enough to learn that, by October 15th, the salmon lying on the riverbanks would be thinned out. Most of the bears would move into the Ray Mountains at this point. Those that didn't, Stan and Charlotte hunted.

By now, Stan had perfected his bear bacon recipe. He would butcher the meat, rub salt and sugar on the fattiest pieces, add a few layers of the same, and compress them in a large rough-cut wooden box, down in the cool air of the root cellar. This process was repeated twice over the course of two weeks. The final touch took only one day of smoking, and of course, a little frying. The resulting product was sweet, savory, and fatty. It was a great way to stock up on energy for the winter.

The grizzlies found in Alaska's interior certainly weren't the biggest on the planet, but it wasn't size that was the concern. Whether a three hundred or five hundred pound grizzly pinned a person down, death would soon follow.

One thing that seemed to set all grizzly bears apart from the other species in the family was their incredible endurance. To offer a comparison: there was a black bear, once, loitering at the standard sand bar that could be seen from the cabin window. Stan took his time, lined up a good shot, and snapped its spine with one bullet. The black bear dropped to the ground. By sheer chance, the very next day, a grizzly bear was walking along the same sandbar, looking for salmon. Stan took the same shot, snapping its spine. The bear broke into a wild sprint, using only its front legs. If Stan had been within twenty-five feet of the bear, though it had lost the use of its lower body, it would have closed the gap before he could have reloaded or turned to retreat. Needless to say, by the time Stan was attacked by a grizzly in the fall of 1976, he was taking them very seriously.

Fishing was coming to a close, and so Stan set out on his annual search for beaver lodges. Cartography had become a crucial part of this process. In autumn, Stan would draw crude maps and mark the various lodges he discovered. In the springtime, during trapping and hunting season, the map would bring him straight to the meat and fur.

On this particular scouting mission, he had three first-year pups with him, off leash and out for a stroll. For defense, he was carrying his .338 magnum. It had a broken magazine spring, so getting one round in the chamber was iffy; a second shot was even less likely without turning the gun upside down and shaking it. It was not the best gun for defense, but replacement parts weren't in his budget, or mindset. The regular protocol meant leaving Charlotte with the .303. So, in accordance with the phrase that could be used to describe absolutely every item and piece of gear in Stan's life, it was *better than nothing.*

As he walked, Stan observed a few uncomfortably large footprints in the soil, but that was typical for that time of year. The real concerning detail was, they were wet, and fresh. Earlier that day, the dogs had been zipping all around him, back and forth through the woods. Now, they were tired and just trudging along in front of him. Stan and the puppy pack crossed the river via sandbar and came around the corner. About four hundred yards away stood three grizzly bears. There was something strange about them. They seemed incredibly active for this time of day. Stan was worried they had picked up his scent and were already agitated by his presence. Docile bears were great; eating bears were busy, but agitated bears were big trouble.

Having never dropped a grizzly in less than two shots, and carrying a gun that could give him one at best, he decided defending himself against three grizzlies just didn't seem wise, no matter how high the potential bacon yield. There was no need for serious alarm yet, though. In fact, the moments that followed were very casual. He decided to simply climb up a tree and taking some time to look at his map of local beaver lodges.

He turned to back off and, just like dock workers waiting for the whistle to blow, his tired dogs assumed this meant it was time to go home. They perked up and took off towards the cabin. They would eventually notice the human leader of the pack was missing and turn around, but the one-minute loss proved to be almost fatal. Stan made it about 10 feet up his tree of choice when he heard snorting and thumping from somewhere nearby. Paws pounded against the soil like a drum. It was a sound more intense than he had imagined in his younger axe-training days. Fortunately, that strategy had long since been abandoned.

While climbing, he turned to see a grizzly about thirty yards off. It was running broadside to him, not charging directly towards him, as he had feared. Stan had his gun in his hand but was unable to take a shot from his place on the tree. He went back to climbing, fast.

Then he heard a rhythmic sort of grunting. It was the sound of air being forced out of the grizzly's lungs by its own massive weight, with each heavy step of its swift run. The sound seemed to grow louder with every second. He couldn't see the bear, but knew it was now charging straight for him.

Before he could even reach for the next branch, he felt the grizzly hit the base of the tree. It came right up at him. His mind completely abandoned registering anything in its natural speed, order, or focus.

The rifle was facing the wrong damn way. Upwards, not down. Stan's first reaction was to push the butt of the rifle down towards the bear, just to put anything between his leg and its jaws. The grizzly sunk its teeth into the stock of the gun, cracked it in two, and pulled it out of Stan's hands.

With Stan's gun in its jaws, the titan fell back to the ground. The force of the pull had thrown off Stan's climbing, and cost him some much needed time. He reached for the next branch, but before he could even pull up, the grizzly was up the tree and on him again. Stan had nothing left to put between him and the grunting monster.

Many people see their lives flash before their eyes in moments like this. Though he didn't see his entire, crazy life, Stan was granted a terrible flash of thought that told him exactly what was going to happen.

He had heard of people being mauled, crippled, and killed by grizzly bears. He had read about it and heard cautionary tales, time and time again.

And now it's going to happen to me, he thought.

He felt a numbness in his leg.

He felt his arms forced skyward by branches.

It was as if the tree had suddenly blasted off to be with the clouds. Regardless of sensation, the grizzly was pulling him out of the tree by his leg.

After that, Stan's memory hit pause, and the recording ceased. An unknown segment of time skipped by, and suddenly he was curled up, somewhere, in the fetal position. He opened his eyes.

There was a bright light above him, and darkness below.

He saw something else.

Bubbles.

Somehow there were bubbles rising up all around him, as if he was a drunken character in a Disney cartoon. This was no dream or hallucination, though. Stan was three feet under water. The cold river had snapped his mind back into focus.

He surfaced, taking in air and wiping the liquid from his eyes all at once. The water was deep here, and it was pushing him down stream. He looked in the direction of his travel to see he was being brought directly towards the two other bears that he had seen earlier. From here he could see they had been cubs all along, only two years old. This explained their mother's aggressive behavior. In a way, Stan respected the mother's response. He had shot countless bears for being near his cabin. It was only right that she should defend her own territory. He immediately realized that if the current carried him much closer, he would likely be in for another visit from momma bear.

He swam to the opposite riverbank and came to an exhausted, pained rest. It was time to assess the situation. He was alive, which was pretty great. The tree he had been ripped out of now stood above him, just over the riverbank. The .338 was still up there, assuming the bear hadn't swallowed it whole just for hate's sake. Stan knew he still had a great deal of grizzly country to make it through before he was safe, and his leg was pretty well out of commission. He looked down and saw strands of red seeping out of his wounded knee and whisking into the clear river water. He could try to make a break for his gun, but couldn't see up and over the bank, and therefore had no idea what horrors awaited him there. For whatever reason, Stan had been spared, and he had no intention of putting himself within the bear's crosshairs again. The gun would remain there until another day.

Then, better late than never, Stan's dogs returned to him, tails wagging, playfully shaking water from their fur after a pleasant swim. Although they were pups, if they hadn't turned to go home exactly when they did, they would have distracted the bear long enough for Stan to get a clean shot off. Instead, they were now one step behind playing the old movie role of the cavalry that shows up just in the nick of time.

He was eight miles down river from his cabin, but only two up from Jack and Karen's. It was a long walk to make with a stiff and bleeding leg. Still, he felt lucky to have friends in reach at all. Karen, among her skills of whit and memory, had a small amount of first aid experience. A streak of pain cut through Stan's knee, and he decided to get moving.

He crawled up the riverbank opposite the scene of the crime. After a quick survey, he became confident that he was not in immediate danger, rose to his feet, and set out walking. He limped through the woods, and out into open tundra. All the while, the dogs were trailing behind. With every single step, his knee grew stiffer, slowing him down and clouding his mind with pain. It was another moment that beckoned Stan's mantra, which he repeated to himself throughout the walk.

Perseverance furthers.

Rather than steep in anger at the misfortune that had beset him, Stan chose to focus on his incredible luck. His leg could have been broken. His face could have been caved in by the swipe of a claw. Instead, he had escaped with only a leg wound, though how severe he wouldn't know for a while. Instead of being stranded fifteen miles from help, he was only two. Stan counted his blessings over the next hour and a half, and then, never too soon, saw land that he recognized. Jack Bloom's dogs started barking first. With the sound of the old homesteader alarm system, Jack stepped out to greet him.

"Oh, hey, Stanley! How ya doing?" Jack, as usual, was happy to see company. He was likely hoping for the customary coffee and insightful talk.

"Doing alright."

As Stan limped closer, Jack saw that the young man was far from it.

"What's with the leg?"

"Oh, I just got bit by a bear."

It was as if Stan experienced an excess of "laid back" in his hippy days, and the rollover was still paying off. He underplayed everything, in part because he hated the idea of unsettling anyone's day. Jack made Stan repeat himself again before the words really sank in.

Jack brought Stan inside, grabbed his gun and walked right back out of the cabin. Stan listened from inside, as Jack's firearm started shouting.

Two miles downriver, Bill Fliris the craftsman and Tom Fogg the survivor perked up. One shot. They stopped what they were doing. Two shots, they gave each other a glance. Three. They flew into motion.

In Tozi speak, three shots meant only one thing: emergency. If by chance, someone were to inadvertently fire three shots at either an animal or target, they were required to immediately sound off a fourth, even though it meant a wasted bullet. There was no mistaking Jack's signal.

The water was damn-near too shallow to travel on. Fortunately, Bill had a riverboat with a forty horsepower jet motor on it. The jet would provide less power; but with no propeller to scrape the gravel below, it would function in skinnier waters.

While Tom and Bill got ready to move out, Karen did her best to patch Stan up. The help was limited to cleaning the wound and providing painkillers. Jack and Karen were prepared for emergencies, but frontier medicine was not going to be enough in this case. Stan needed a hospital. He eagerly waited for the painkillers to kick in, and received over a half hour of Tozi medical care before Bill and Tom came careening around the riverbend, right up to Jack and Karen's property.

Since the bush rescue team arrived prepared for any situation, Jack quickly gave them the break down. They didn't need guns, and the first-aid was taken care of. All they needed to do was haul ass down river, to Tanana.

As Stan was lifted into the boat, he realized that Charlotte had no way of knowing what had happened. Before Stan could voice this concern, Jack offered to make the eight-mile walk up to see Charlotte.

The three men rattled off their knowledge of the river ahead. The speed wasn't just a matter of urgency. It was the only way they could complete the journey. If the boat slowed too much, it would fall off step, and sink too low into the water. The more this happened, the more the boat would bottom out, and the more time would be lost unloading it, and dragging it to deeper waters.

With Stan laying flat in the boat, Tom and Bill took off as if launched by an aircraft carrier. Bill kept the throttle sky high and steered with precision, while Tom sat on the bow, his eyes darting back and forth, searching for sandbars, sweepers, and any other obstacles that stood in their way.

Each of the Tozi homesteaders had a good knowledge base on where to watch out for sandbars, but the river's current kept the blockages in a constant state of movement and shifting. No level of experience could accurately predict where the water's depth would go from five inches, to one.

Sweepers were even harder to predict. Freshly fallen trees were common all along the river, and most were low enough to knock the top console and any upright passengers right off of a boat.

The craft crashed, skipped, and flew right over sandbars and gravel. They hit river bends at full speed, and the boat wanted to roll as it whipped around wide, sliding and drifting impossibly close to the riverbank. Stan, laying on the boat's floor, could only listen to the mania while watching treetops pass them by.

"Holy shit, here comes another one!" Someone yelled, and they crashed through stony riffles so hard that the outboard motor kicked upward into the air, completely out of the water. Stan heard the engine do a dry scream before Bill forced it downward into a gurgle.

Immediately after the motor was returned to the water, another river bend sprung up in front of them. It was too sudden and too sharp. The boat wrecked upward, head first, onto the bank. Bill and Tom jumped to their feet and began prying the trusty craft back into the water. Then they were off again, full speed ahead.

A few river bends later, the bow of the boat smashed into what seemed like an invisible sandbar. The bar was too high, and too long.

Sand screeched and scratched along the hull, and the boat, now a battering ram, grinded to a halt. It was high centered. Tom and Bill stepped out onto the sand to push while Stan stuck to his job; lying in the bottom of the boat. By now, his system was flooded with downers and painkillers from all walks of life. He was feeling no pain, that much was certain. The drugs had a strange effect on Stan's ego and empathy, and he quickly started barking out orders to his rescuers as if they were dogs. It was not the last time the boat would get stuck, and Stan had enough sass to get them all the way down the Tozi River.

The men heaved with everything they had, and eventually resolved that the boat needed to be even lighter. They lifted Stan out of the boat and let him rest on the sandbar. A thin sheet of water greeted him, soaking his clothes. Slowly, the hull was dragged into deeper waters. Stan was loaded back into the boat, and the journey continued.

The craft strafed around endless corners, and Stan saw it all from a reverse bird's eye view. Eventually, there came another shout.

"SWEEPER!"

It was a fallen birch tree, stretched across the river, three feet above the water. Bill didn't even have time to try stopping the boat.

"Get down!"

The tree forced the front end of the boat beneath it, deep into the water, and everyone lurched forward. It scraped further back along the hull, producing the high-pitched squeak of wet wood on metal. Thin branches whipped and smacked the riverboat's exhausted crew. Tom was knocked down, right on top of Stan, who called out:

"My leg!"

In seconds, the tree swept from bow to stern, and smacked directly into the boat's console, ripping it off. Bill called out:

"My console!"

The boat stopped dead. The sudden halt threw the men forward even further. Though the boat stopped, its wake had not, and deep rolls of pursuing water lapped up and over the back of the craft, swamping it.

They offloaded again, and set to work on bailing out the flood of water, needing to at least get the boat light enough to continue its painful journey down the Tozi. By the time the bucket of a boat was empty, the painkillers had lost their effect on Stan. The hurt kicked in, first like thunder, then lightning. He became increasingly aware of the blood that he was losing. As he lay in the bottom of the boat, seeing mostly trees and sky drift by, feeling the boat bank hard, he could hear his friends navigating the narrow waters.

"Swing left! Cut right! Bar! Watch it, watch it!"

Finally, they broke out onto the open waters of the Yukon. The normally lengthy cruise along the Yukon became jetliner-fast. The motor red-lined in a straight shot up to Tanana.

Tom and Bill helped Stan up the riverbank to the hospital. As if right out of a sixties horror film, when the nurse that greeted them took a look at pale, ragged, bleeding Stan, she actually screamed.

While they worked on Stan, the doctors put in a call to Fairbanks for a bear specialist. They carried on a phone conversation, all while examining, cleaning, and treating Stan's wound. During this call, they learned how truly lucky Stan had been. Although the bear's canine teeth were only an inch and a half long, the hole went three full inches under Stan's kneecap. It was a compression bite. Six times the depth that Bray Maloney had managed with his knife a lifetime ago in the alley outside of the Boston theater that had just concluded its showing of *West Side Story.*

This wound, by tooth rather than knife, could have been far worse than it already was. If the bear had shaken Stan, whipped him into a ragdoll, or dragged him, she would have ripped his kneecap clean off. Instead of a killing assault, the bear had seemingly opted to bite, release, and leave Stan with only a scar to remember her by. He had either lost consciousness from his fall out of the tree, and been rolled down the bank by his attacker, or made a terrified, limping run and tumble into the water. These were the best and only theories. After that bite, how Stan had actually managed his way down the riverbank and into the water would forever remain a mystery.

After Stan was treated, he was taken to Ken Lilly's house to relax and recover. Ken was another lieutenant in the army of generous people that contributed to Stan and Charlotte's way of living. He wasn't home, but the rescuers knew he wouldn't mind. Ken showed up later to find Stan laying in his bed, high on morphine.

Meanwhile, Jack had returned up river to Stan's cabin. He needed to let Charlotte know what happened to her boyfriend, but he rarely visited in the summer and wasn't entirely sure how to find the place. As the sun set, he called out into the forest, in the hopes of being heard.

"CHARLOTTE!" his deep voice boomed through the trees.

No response.

"CHARLOTTE!"

Nothing. Jack reluctantly decided to camp, knowing that he would have much better luck in the morning. He had no way of knowing, but Charlotte had actually heard his call. Normally, whenever Stan returned home from a long trip, he would call out with a distant, high-pitched "Yahoo!" to let her know that he was close. Charlotte assumed that Jack's call had been Stan's, and as per usual, didn't respond.

Painful hours passed for Charlotte, and her mind raced. She couldn't fathom how Stan could have made it so close to home, but not finished the final stretch. What followed was one of the worst nights of Charlotte's life, far worse than Stan's bear attack and subsequent boat ride of pain. In her mind, it was a certainty: Stan had been attacked and killed by a bear.

She grabbed a gun, and rushed out into the night with the dogs for protection. She was searching for a pair of legs, sticking out from behind some bushes, belonging to a man that had been half eaten by a monster.

Her search nearly brought her to Jack's camp, which would have cleared the entire issue up. Instead, by chance and misfortune, she turned back to the cabin, and spent a miserable night trying to accept the fact that Stan had died a gruesome death.

The next day, Jack walked out onto the sand bar that could be seen through the cabin's window. Charlotte ran outside, and right away, Jack yelled to her.

"Stanley's alright!"

"Where is he?" Charlotte called back, not yet convinced that *anything* was alright.

"We got drunk and played cards last night," he shouted. "I won a hand and got you, so here I am!"

Hearing Jack's humor made her feel better than anything else. Then he crossed the river and told her what really happened, and the joke was over.

On day three of Stan's stay in Tanana, Ken Lilly came home and went into an uproar.

"Alright," he said. "You smell worse than usual today."

Stan had been lying in the house all day, so he hadn't noticed it. Ken sniffed him; he wasn't the source. After digging around, he found Stan's pants, which had been cut off at the hospital. They had been sitting, balled up in a corner, soaked in water, slime from an entire summer of cutting fish, and blood from Stan's wound.

Ken tossed the pants outside, and the scent of the household slowly returned to normal. Twelve days later, as Stan was leaving his house for a return to his homestead, he scooped the jeans back up again. A good pair of pants was hard to come by on the Tozi River.

> *"When you think of the times I've truly killed*
> *how could I truly hate*
> *one who has injured only slightly*
> *only me."*

-Stan's Poem, written after the bear attack

Though the stock of Stan's .338 Magnum has been almost seamlessly epoxied back into one piece, the mark of the grizzly bear's tooth remains deeply ingrained in the wood.

The Ballad of The Grizzly

A Folk Song Written by Stan Zuray

To a tune and rhythm similar but not identical to "The Times They are a-Changin'," by Bob Dylan. Accompanied by guitar.

The fish start jumpin' and the birds hit the breeze
And I'm so scared, my legs start to freeze
Alone, out walkin' my three dogs and me.
On up ahead what's that my eyes they do see.

It's three big grizzlies and they're startin' to run
I wish it was but it don't look like for fun
They're mean old creatures may they come after me
Just to be safe think I'll sit in a tree

Where's a good tree I think there's one over there
From up in that I'll blast the hair off those bears
No need to hurry branches catch in my hair
But what's that sound in them bushes right there

It's one of them grizzlies and she's movin' my way
Home fishin' for salmon that's where I should have stay.
When I woke up it seemed like such a nice day
Safe in my bed I wish my body now lay.

That mean rotten bear bit me right in the knee
For a few seconds seemed like my mind couldn't see
Woke up in the water and looked back by the tree

I's so happy no grizzlies come swimming with me

Swim cross the river head for the tundra real fast
So far ok and maybe the feeling won't last
And here's my dogs they comin' over to me
I got a feelin' they didn't even see

Through all sorts of tangle head for the sun in the south
Wash of some blood with some spit from my mouth
It don't look too bad but now stiffer than hell
I look towards the bluffs wishin' I could maybe yell

A mile across the tundra, and I hit the dry slough
I'm comin' home momma tuck me in bed when you're through
No need to worry when lots of people around
Someone will help you when you're down on the ground

And now things are better I'm getting around
I ain't learned too much but so far I have found
That I just want to spend my life
Up on the Tozi without any strife
I just want a life to love
Far from those roads and close to above.

Chapter 15

Crock

June, 1976.

Stan Zuray was a man of vision, there's no denying that. He had dreams, possessed the determination to accomplish them, and the mental flexibility to adapt his plans as he went. However, it's important to declare that not all of his ideas were foolproof.

As Stan drove his dogs across the vast tundra, he imagined how perfect it might be to be joined by a falcon companion that partnered with him in his hunting endeavors. He imagined sending the great bird of prey upward, from forearm to sky, and watching it sweep and scan the landscape. Perhaps he could train it to circle in the above any moose or caribou that it found. It could even return to him, caw for his attention, and then guide him to the large prey. He knew they were smart birds, so the idea wasn't completely outlandish.

The dream evolved, and one day Stan found himself ordering a book entitled "The Art of Falconry." He poured over the pages, ingesting tip after tip on training and feeding. The book showed diagrams of all the equipment he would need. He took to crafting them with moose hide right away. He made a hood and jesses, which could be strapped to the bird's ankle and assist in training it to fly away only on command.

The project hit a stumbling block once the time came for a crucial piece of the puzzle. Stan did not have a falcon. Two years prior, he had inadvertently caught one in a marten trap. He took it home, fed it, and released it soon after. All of this occurred before he began to truly dream about falconry. Now, although it could happen again, there was no way of immediately procuring one of the birds.

So, as Stan often did, he adjusted his mission to fit the circumstances. There was a raven's nest two miles down river that he had previously encountered while out exploring. He returned to the nest and, despite mother-raven cawing and pecking away at him, Stan managed to safely remove one baby from the nest. Returning to the cabin with the newest member of his animal family, he constructed a tiny, comfortable home. This entailed nailing a wide frying pan, high up onto the top of a post, and covering it with sticks and hay. Amazingly, it took the form of a nest. The baby bird had no problem staying in the nest, and each day Stan climbed his ladder to feed his tiny friend.

Based on his falconry book, he learned that the bird should eat meat that includes either feathers or fur for fiber. This was the suggested diet for a falcon, not a raven, but Stan decided to play it safe and stick with the book's recommendation. Later, with the bird's first call, it received its name.

"CROCK!"

As time went on, Stan continued to take parenting and training advice from the falconry manual. Now the Tozi cabin had a raven that was being raised by a human as if it was a falcon. Undoubtedly, these were very confusing times for Crock and probably Mother Nature herself.

Circumstances aside, training continued and Stan formed a fast friendship with the bird. He successfully trained it to land on his forearm. If he raised the arm perch high, Crock would happily step onto Stan's shoulder and remain there until he was commanded to fly. This stance came with a mixed sense of accomplishment and fear. As fantastic and wonderful as it was to see the training pay off, Stan had also observed ravens eating fish countless times. More often than not, they would pluck out the fish's eyeball first. Now, Stan was strolling around with the big, black beak constantly protruding into his peripheral vision. He was living in terror for a while, but Crock never struck.

The loyal bird would perch on Stan's dog sled for runs along the trapline. It would roam freely all day and consistently return. It was just about time for Stan to begin figuring out the next step: teaching the raven to spot a moose.

In the winter, Stan covered the cabin's windows with semi-transparent plastic for insulation. Crock couldn't see inside, and he hated this. Repeatedly, he pecked and ripped his way through the plastic just to say hello. Even the fish rack was in harm's way. Stan approached numerous times to find the dog food lying on the ground with fresh beak pecks gouged into it. Tools started vanishing from all over the yard. Crock was strong enough to play pranks on Stan now. Shiny things had a tendency to disappear while the bird was loose. Crock's temperament had changed from adorable toddler to teenage rebel.

Eventually, all hopes of training a moose-hunting-raven, as well as ever finding his crescent wrench, were gone. Stan invited Crock onto his sled for one more ride. It would be a long one. Stan traveled all the way into Tanana, and took Crock straight to the dump. There was a regular crowd of ravens that liked to hang around the garbage, so Stan delivered Crock to the social scene, hoping the bird could rejoin his own kind. There, the rebellious raven would have all the food he ever wanted, and perhaps even some bird-to-bird camaraderie.

Back at the cabin, work returned to its usual grind, until two weeks later. Crock shouted his namesake from the trees above Stan. The bird had flown roughly thirty air miles to return to him. Fortunately, Stan knew, as easy as birds were to train, they were even easier to un-train. Stan started shouting, waving his arms, and chasing Crock around the yard. It wasn't enough to break their bond, though. He grabbed a hold of his rifle and fired one warning shot every time Crock came around. Slowly, Stan's black-feathered friend was forced to go wild, and live a life of his own in the wilderness.

It was better this way. Crock needed to be with his own kind, and Stan needed his tools. Stan hadn't seen the bird for the last time, though. During his trips to town, his dogs were often and suddenly spooked when Crock would come out from hiding on the trail and lunge at them while spreading his wings wide. The pranks seemed like they would never end. Slowly though, Crock grew in maturity and the scare tactics stopped. Either that, or he simply grew bored. Still, on many trips between Tanana and the cabin, Stan could look out onto the open tundra and see a low-flying raven keeping pace with the sled and shouting out its namesake from time to time.

Chapter 16
Fording the River

January, 1977.

Stan and Charlotte were married in the warmth of their cabin with the rest of the homesteaders in attendance. Ringo Mclaughlin was the town magistrate at the time. The man who had once delivered a life-altering batch of food to the young homesteaders after their fire was now joining them in holy matrimony.

Though the wedding was largely traditional, the honeymoon was not. Per the typical mad rush of the lifestyle, after the wedding Stan had to hurry his way to town for another crucial supply run. It was a good thing he did, because as he was returning he saw a sight for any homesteader's sore eyes.

Moose were more like statues in the dead of winter, during deep cold. They focused on conserving their energy, saving most of it for body heat. On this particular day, Stan saw one such statue on his way home from the trapline. It was forty degrees below zero, and he knew he had a great chance of bringing this one home. No complaints there; a mid-winter moose was considered a tremendous blessing.

He called the dogs to a halt and started with his customary five-second countdown, hoping to get a shot off before they decided to wildly charge at the food supply. The moose's head was in the sights of Stan's Winchester .338. This was the rifle that had been retrieved and salvaged from the site of the bear attack. It took some epoxy to put the stock back together, but the gun still worked, mostly.

Stan pulled the trigger. The gun clicked. Then came the barking choir, and the moose reluctantly moved off. Stan had known full well by now that the spring driving the firing pin wasn't the strongest in the world's arsenal. It wouldn't have been much to purchase a replacement, but Stan was almost morally opposed to spending money on things that could be fixed. The spring couldn't actually be fixed, as Stan had already tried stretching it; but still, finding the time to find the part in a magazine, call from Tanana, and order it, seemed like such a waste. Excuses aside, the gun had worked pretty well so far.

Fortunately, the moose hadn't taken off at full speed. Fresh, obvious tracks were left behind by the creature; imprinted in deep powder. Stan strapped on his snowshoes and left the sled behind, hoping to catch up to the meal.

The moose had stopped only one hundred feet from its original position. Stan raised his rifle and clicked it at the moose. The animal stared at him, as if waiting for the gun's punch line. Flustered would be an understatement for Stan's state of mind at this juncture. He crouched in the snow, removed the rifle's bolt, tucked it into his parka, and under his armpit. A gun should certainly fire at forty below, but cold was this rifle's Achilles heel. After five minutes of enjoying a staring contest with eight hundred pounds of meat while enduring cold metal under his warmest layer, Stan reassembled the firearm and went for take three. The gun refused to fulfill its destiny yet again. Stan looked into the moose's eyes.

"Don't go anywhere."

He trudged maybe twenty feet to the nearest birch tree. The thin white bark shared many qualities with paper, including density, consistency, and flammability. Once he had enough, Stan crouched down into the snow, struck a match, and created a quick, hot, impromptu fire. He held the bolt directly over the flames, glancing back and forth between the heat and the meat. It only took two minutes to bring the bolt up to a suitable temperature.

Now, for the old process; reassemble, ready, and aim. The spring drove the firing pin into the casing's primer, which caused the propellant to explode, and sent one bullet whizzing out of the barrel. The bullet made its impact, and the fatally patient moose fell to the snow.

Months later, once the food yield from that moose had run out, the snow began to melt, the sun spent more time loitering in the sky, and springtime was around the corner. It was time for beaver trapping. This was a process that normally involved cutting through two feet of ice, inserting a birch pole in the water below, and rigging it with snares to entangle the beavers as they swam towards what looked like an upright meal. At this particular lodge, though, Stan encountered a bizarre phenomenon. Once he cut his way through two feet of ice, he found not water, but air. Ptarmigan Creek had frozen over in fall time, when water levels were higher. Over the course of the cold winter, the water beneath had drained out until nothing remained. It was a hollow creek.

Stan dropped down the hole and into a bizarre cave, made half of ice and half of dry creek bed. He crawled through the odd space, lit by the dim sunlight that had been filtered through a groaning ceiling of ice, which hovered four feet above the ground.

The space was unique, beautiful, and utterly terrifying. Stan could see places where the ice had already cracked and collapsed inward. He also knew that, upstream, the spring melt had arrived, and it was only a matter of time before the overflow made its way down to him. He wondered how much time he would have once the water started flowing into this space. He scurried along the creek bed, by no means taking his time.

Stan was no longer trying to snare swimming beavers. Instead, he would have to trap them as they walked. Once he found the beavers' feed pile, he set leg hold traps and made his escape. The ice did not collapse, but Stan would not be receiving any food or fur from this particular set. The next day, he returned to his hole in the ice to check the traps. The overflow had advanced further downstream, but hadn't yet hit his trapping hole. He climbed down to take a look.

The traps were empty, and he debated whether or not he should leave them for another day. He decided to pull them, which turned out to be a very wise decision. Only two hours later, he returned to find the chasm filled to the brim with flowing water.

During beaver trapping season, ice caves such as this were a rare, but not unheard of product of the spring melt. There was another, more bothersome, seasonal river condition that occurred without fail each year. The significantly swifter Tozi River was an even larger source of beaver meat, and the mid-river ice consistently collapsed and melted first, leaving behind a shelf of ice on either riverbank. This made fording the river by dog sled a tremendous hassle.

Stan reluctantly approached his first river crossing in these conditions, hoping for some good luck. The dogs loyally charged down the shelf ice, and into the frigid waters. Their paws barely touched the river's bottom as they pulled the sled into the river. By the time Stan was wet up to his knees, the dogs were pulling exclusively by swimming. Stan's only goal was to keep the water levels below his thighs.

The whole operation was steadily pushed downriver as the dogs struggled to make it to the other side. Slowly they regained their footing, climbed up onto the opposite shelf ice, and started pulling. The dogs made it. The sled did not. As the front bumper caught the edge of the ice, the entire team was yanked to a halt. The river's current rushed into the broadside of the sled, forcing it to pivot, and roll over. Any item or piece of gear that wasn't secured to the sled was dumped into the river. This included Stan.

He waded through the cold waters, which were now above his waist, and attempted to get the sled upright, but there wasn't enough slack on the line between it and the dog team. Stan yanked on the line, trying to shift the team from "park," to "reverse," but they refused, instead going into "drive," and further pinning the sled's bumper against the ice. Though it was a loyal team, they saw absolutely no reason why they should have to return for an encore swim.

After five minutes of struggling, swearing, and gradually numbing his legs, Stan managed to bring the sled's bumper above the ice. He commanded the dogs to pull it out of the water, and they did.

Due to the tight, consecutive bends of the Tozi River, this fording process would have to be completed twelve times per trapline run. Eighty-four times per week.

Out of necessity and frustration, innovation eventually struck. One fine day, Stan brought his team to a halt at the first river crossing of his trip. He tightly secured two empty gas jugs to the front of his sled, gave his dogs a few extra ounces of attention and love, turned to regard the water once more, and then took his position.

"UH-kay!"

The dogs took off, down the riverbank, across the shelf ice, and plunged into the water. They kicked off of the riverbed until it was out of reach, then the swimming began. Stan pressed down on his handle, keeping his waist above water and kicking with his legs to provide extra thrust. The back of the sled sank like a stone, but the front end floated like a "cool breeze." The lead dogs climbed up onto the ice. They pulled up the swing dogs, which in turn yanked the wheel dogs out of the water. The floating nose of the sled landed just above the defending shelf ice, and the dogs pulled both vehicle and driver out of the river. It was frontier waterskiing, and worked wonders for trapline efficiency, as well as Stan's mental wellbeing.

The Earth took another sixty spins, and summer arrived. Along with it came new tasks, fewer sled rides, and more mosquitos. The banks of the Tozitna River had been shifting closer to the cabin every year since Stan and Charlotte arrived. From a raven's-eye-view, over time, the river would create the image of a snake slithering in place. Perhaps the young couple had a few more years, but waiting until the last minute was to be avoided at all costs. It was time to move. Of course, unlike the average move, there wasn't a new structure waiting to receive their furniture. Moving in this context meant literally moving the entire cabin.

They marked each log of the cabin, based on which side it faced, and its position in the stack. *N, S, E, W,* then *1, 2, 3,* 4, and so on. They dug a new root cellar, laid a new gravel foundation and slowly, log by log, relocated their entire home log for log, with one difference: they took the opportunity to upgrade from dirt floor to wood.

That summer they were hit by an unprecedented amount of rain, and the Tozi River flooded. It was fortunate that they had been prudent about moving their cabin, but the flood's most disastrous effects wouldn't strike for another four years.

The next task was, finally, digging a well. The depth of the root cellar had taken Stan eight feet closer to the water table. He would need to make it down to twenty if he wanted to have flowing water throughout the winter. He started digging.

One, two, three, four feet to start. He cut the ends off of a fifty-five gallon drum and inserted it into the hole to keep the sides of gravel from caving in. Then came more digging. Finally, he pounded pipe into the ground by hand, and struck cool, delicious, clear spring water. The times of shuffling five gallon buckets to and from the river were over.

The farming and gardening operation had completely exploded by this point. Over the course of years, Stan had ground up tundra that was often frozen even in the summer, and turned it into an enormous two hundred by fifty foot farm for vegetables and wheat. It was a job that kept him busy in the early and later summer days.

Thanks to the ever-generous men of The Site, another improvement came in. Stan was gifted a CB radio, which may not have been much use if not for the illegal one hundred watt amplifier that came with it. Stan attached a thirty-foot tall antenna to the closest spruce tree, and got to work on creating his generator. Combining a small, two horsepower gas engine taken from a washing machine motor, an alternator from the Tanana junkyard, and a twelve-volt car battery, Stan was able to bring electricity to the Tozi cabin for the first time. To maintain power for the radio, the battery only needed charging once every two weeks, so the quiet nature of the homestead remained intact, without the constant hum of his homemade generator.

There was one other hunk of technology that Stan had reluctantly acquired. Snow machines were far from dependable in the seventies, and often broke down. This ordinarily wouldn't have been much deterrent for a gearhead like Stan. The real issue was, he simply didn't like them. Still, the machine would be a time-saver, so perhaps it would be worth the noise and exhaust.

Rather than taking his dogs into town for his supply run, Stan tried out his new snow machine. The trip was faster; that was undeniable, but the engine was obnoxiously loud, the ride was bumpy, and the smell of exhaust caught up with him every time he stopped. On the return journey of that trip, Stan made up his mind. If he wanted to move freight by this method, he might as well move back to Boston and get into the trucking business. Exhaust and noise were not things he had been seeking that day in seventy-three when he was dropped off on the river. The snow machine would remain a mere emergency option, and a mechanical migraine for only another year and a half before Stan sold it and fully returned to the way of dog and sled.

There were a few other seldom but regular interruptions in the quiet peace. Military aircraft continued to make swooping dives into the valley and crash their way through the sound barrier above, each time igniting Tom Fogg's self-preservation instincts from his times overseas.

Even more often, helicopters would touch down on the killing sandbar outside of Stan's cabin. This was the bush equivalent to a stranger rolling down their window and asking for directions. These were days when paper maps were king, not GPS. Stan's knowledge of the region's geography only expanded, and some pilots came to rely on it.

During one such visit, Stan heard the familiar sound of rotor blades spinning down and stepped outside to meet the pilot, ready to inform him on how to find whatever he was looking for. Before the blades quit spinning, an Air Force lieutenant sprang from the cabin and sprinted towards Stan. In one hand, the lieutenant held a large medical kit, in the other: a blanket.

Before Stan could say hello, the lieutenant ran right past him and up towards the cabin. Stan looked back at the pilot in the chopper, but received no clues as to what the hell was going on. So he gave chase after the lieutenant, running at full speed behind him, and hoping to find out what kind of medical emergency had cropped up in the cabin without him knowing about it.

By the time Stan made it inside, he walked into a heated discussion between the lieutenant and Charlotte. The chopper had landed at the wrong cabin. Downriver, Karen had been pregnant for about eight months. Her due date was rapidly approaching. Amidst the confusion, Stan learned that she had gone into labor early. He returned to the chopper with the now fuming lieutenant and gave him directions.

"Down river about seven air miles to the confluence of the Tozitna River and Dag Creek, turn south, first house on the left."

As the lieutenant climbed back into his bird, Stan got the impression that the pilot was on his way to a court martial just as soon as the baby was brought into the world. Either that, or he would have latrine duty for the rest of his career.

Downriver, before the helicopter even arrived, young Robin Bloom was born. Despite the premature labor occurring miles from any hospital, she was in good health. Stan and Charlotte agreed that, if it ever came to a baby of their own, they would have to play it safe and spend one month in advance in Tanana, just to be sure.

As luck would have it, that month in Tanana was right around the corner.

Stan and his dogs in front of the cabin. Summer, 1977.

Stan plants potatoes on a patch of tundra that was once black spruce forest. Trees were removed with an axe and come along, and the earth was churned up so it could thaw in the summer.

Chapter 17
The Hospital

March, 1978.

Charlotte was already eight months pregnant. By now, they had purchased an old run-down trailer, installed a stove, and created a home away from home in Tanana. The increased frequency of their visits had brought an end to couch surfing, as neither one of them wanted to be a continued burden on the locals. Though Ken Lilly, Joe Runyon, and the boys at The Site would happily have continued to help.

Charlotte went into labor in the Tanana hospital, just as the sun was setting on a spring day. What started as a standard delivery suddenly changed into a collection of concerned looks from the doctor and nurse. Something was wrong. The baby had slowed down somewhere along his journey through the birth canal. Worse, his heart rate was weakening. A C-section would be risky in the small village hospital, and a medevac was called out of Fairbanks.

After two hours of waiting, mother, father, and nurse were loaded onto the plane. This was when Stan was given the brunt of the news. The chances of the baby surviving the next two hours were slim. The chief concern now was saving Charlotte's life.

Things moved fast from there, from runway to ambulance to hospital. A C-section was performed, but it was too late. The baby had been coming out feet first, wrapped in his umbilical cord. The doctors brought Stan and Charlotte their son, wrapped in blankets. After saying goodbye to the newborn that would never grow old, Stan and Charlotte watched as he was taken away. It was a pain more difficult than any winter blow or starvation had ever caused them.

Three days later, Stan and Charlotte were on their way back to Tanana, carrying the ashes of their forever-young son.

Chapter 18

Monica

Word had spread fast in the small town, and the couple was received with a flood of condolences and sympathy. They were surrounded by friends and support.

Both Stan and Charlotte were in the Tanana general store when life took a turn for the strange and beautiful. Marion Joseph, a Tanana local and Alaskan native, approached them. She started with an outpouring of sympathy, and then explained something that would alter the course of their lives. Marion's daughter, Sandra, had just given birth, but was too young to care for the child. Sandra had planned on going to school and building a stable life before starting a family; but life had not unfolded that way. She asked the young homesteaders if they would be interested in adopting the baby.

That night, Stan and Charlotte returned to their trailer, started a fire, and questioned what they would do. On one hand, it seemed terribly wrong. They would be adopting a baby amidst the emotional turmoil of losing another. Giving time to heal seemed essential to the process. On the other side, it seemed like an adoption that could benefit everyone. Young Sandra would go to school, and Stan and Charlotte would have the joy of raising a child amidst the trees, rivers and animals. By the end of the night, together they reached a decision. They couldn't think of a single reason why they shouldn't at least visit Sandra and Marion in their home.

From there, the start of a family was inevitable. Stan and Charlotte immediately fell in love with baby Monica. One week later, the Zuray dog sled was scraping its way north on what little snow remained, carrying mother, father, and child.

Later that year, once the sun was consistently high and the ground thawed, Stan and Charlotte hiked north of the cabin, carrying baby Monica. At the end of Charlotte's trapline, within the foothills of the Ray Mountains, sat a gorgeous, wide-open lake and a small cabin that the couple had constructed on a hill, overlooking the water. There, they buried the ashes of their first born, held a private funeral, and placed a white birch cross over the grave. The walk back was somber, with peaks of levity added in by baby Monica's occasional coo.

Monica's childhood was, as anyone might guess, outrageously unique. With Jack and Karen having baby Robin, plus Russ Wood's wife, Anne, giving birth to Iris; there were now three children on the Tozitna River. Still, as per typical travel restrictions, the kids rarely saw each other. This meant Monica was often without playmate; but what she was lacking that department was made up for tenfold with dogs.

Two years had passed since the Zurays lost one child and gained another. They had healed as much as anyone could after such a turn in life's winding trail. As Monica was putting her newfound walking ability to good use, one of the dogs had given birth to a healthy litter. Baby Monica walked and crawled over to the doghouse that contained the mother and her young, future-sled dogs. Monica's tiny hands gripped the dog's collar, yanked, and pulled for as long as it took. Eventually, reluctantly, the mother stepped out of her own home, feeling evicted. Baby Monica crawled into the house and spent most of her day cuddling with eight tiny puppies. This would soon become a daily ritual.

All the while, as Monica was gearing up for childhood, another treasured member of the Zuray family was growing old. Skipper was twelve by now, the rough equivalent to seventy-two human years. One of his eyes had started to fog over, and he simply couldn't pull a sled like he used to. Stan had long since relieved the large and loyal dog from the more difficult journeys to town, though the old-timer was still occasionally harnessed up with other dogs for short hauls around the cabin property. Activity and exercise were still helpful in keeping the dog's tail wagging. During one such chore, Stan enlisted the help of Skipper and two others to pull some firewood back to the cabin.

"UH-kay," came the command, but Skipper simply stood at attention. Stan shouted again, the two assisting dogs yanked, Skipped didn't so much as look back. Stan gave the wolf dog a whack on his rear, and received a growl in return. He realized then that the bear fighting, life saving, keen sensing, toughest dog he ever knew had just decided he had done enough work for one lifetime. The wolf in him allowed for the defiance, and Stan didn't fight him on it. Skipper wasn't dying, not yet, but he was retiring.

As Skipper entered his final years, a new star was quickly rising through the ranks of the team. Two generations prior, a dog mushing legend had gifted Stan a litter of puppies with thick and healthy fur, perfect for bitter cold runs on the trapline. George Attla was not only a legend, but Stan's hero, making the puppies incredibly special. Meanwhile, Monica's grandfather had given Stan a half German Shepard, affectionately named Dumbo. The two bloodlines merged. Grizzly was born of that mating, who was a great dog herself, but it was her son that was truly special.

Thus entered Chumper, a dog that was essentially descended from royalty. He by no means possessed Skipper's stature, but grew to have incredible strength and a mind that never ceased to marvel Stan. The dog-prodigy was leading Stan's team by the time he was one year old.

There were days, once every three or four years, where the entire Alaskan interior opened up to Stan and his team. After three days and nights of perfect temperatures, the snow would melt during the day without re-freezing at night. When it finally did freeze, the resulting crust of ice was thick enough to support a sled. This meant that instead of sticking to the hard pack of an existing trail, or burning out the dogs by dragging a sled through deep powder, absolutely everywhere in sight was fair game to travel.

Chumper's intelligence made this open form of exploring both simple and fun. Stan could call "gee," and Chumper would steer the team right, "haw," and he would turn left. Whereas some leaders might have trouble roaming open hills without a trail to follow, Chumper could catch the subtlest variations in Stan's voice, and adjust course accordingly.

These days were like open sea travel, and Stan often took advantage of them by heading up into the Ray Mountains to enjoy the vast and endless slopes. Amidst all the work that his life entailed, this was a treasured form of pure recreation. He took the team out simply for the fun of it, and to explore parts of the wilderness that he might otherwise never have seen.

The former greaser and car-thief kicked, called, and smiled all throughout the Ray Mountain Range, knowing that he was the only human for miles. The views were incredible and the freedom was boundless. There was not a single sound apart from Stan's own voice, the panting dogs, and the soft whoosh of the sled gliding across the hardened snow.

Just like Skipper, Chumper's personality and abilities proved to not only be fun, but life saving. Once, Stan was high up in the Ray Mountains with a Tanana friend by the name of Chuck Hugny. The two stood high on a mountain and looked down into a valley that they immediately wanted to explore. The journey down appeared steep, but manageable. It would be more like skiing than mushing, which was so much the better.

Stan took the lead and commenced the most amazing and terrifying ride of his life. He quickly noticed that his speed was picking up to something between dog sled and hotrod. The downward slope beneath his feet increased, and he suddenly realized he could only see fifty feet ahead before the horizon dropped off. The sled's speed surpassed any previous record that Stan had set. Ahead, he could now see that the dogs were more falling than running down the mountain.

Looking beyond Chumper to the approaching horizon, Stan saw an outcropping of rocks jutting out of the snow. He had seen enough terrain to know exactly what this meant; the rocks marked the top of a cliff, where below, more rocks were waiting. Both Stan and Chuck slammed down on their brakes, and thick, tall rooster tails of powder kicked up behind them. Stan's team, without footing, continued what was essentially a free-fall towards the ledge, through a foot and a half of powder.

It was a hill so steep, and so socked in with snow, that simply walking up it would have been nearly impossible. Even asking the dogs to stand still and upright without tumbling over would have been a task. The idea of stopping so much momentum was an absolute pipe dream.

"HAW! HAW! HAW!" Stan put his vocal chords through scratchy pain.

Chumper heard the urgency in Stan's voice, and somehow, having only been born a year and a half prior, found his footing where the rest of the team could not. Through the powder that was being kicked up into Stan's face, he could see which dog harnesses had tension. The young pup was pulling the team to the left, completely under his own power. While Stan did his part—shouting and struggling to keep the sled upright—Chumper did his, which was saving the team.

With Chuck's team following Stan's freshly broken trail, the avalanche of dogs slowly deviated course, one degree at a time, and the sled scraped just to the left of the rocks. As the downward slope evened out, Stan allowed himself a brief glimpse back over his shoulder, at what he had so narrowly avoided. It was just as he had feared, a sheer and deadly drop.

Other dogs might not have acknowledged the command so readily. Cleetsa, back in her day, might have happily frolicked off the rocky ledge, hoping to fly or die. Chumper, however, ignored the slope that was too steep for any dog to stand on, and acknowledge Stan's command by arcing the entire team to safety.

Chumper's strength was impressive, but his mind was a total anomaly. Stan once found himself caught beneath the setting sun while far from the trail that would lead him back through the forest and to his cabin. Rather than spend the extra hour backtracking in to find the trail, Stan opted to take the team straight down the mountains and through the trees, back to the cabin. Down in the valley, without the benefit of a trail, the forest was a dense obstacle.

The young pup lead the team through the woods effortlessly. He was threading a needle eight times per minute. From behind, Stan kept up with dodging the various spruce boughs that were attempting to slap him in the face. Chumper dove between a particularly narrow gap between trees and suddenly grinded to a dead stop. Stan had no idea what he had seen or smelled, but hit the brakes anyway, preventing a seven-dog pile up. Chumper reversed course, swung around the two trees, and resumed his run. Stan stopped the sled a second time and examined their original path. The dogs had fit through the narrow gap; but somehow Chumper knew that the sled would not. He prevented an accident that not even Stan saw coming.

The wits and brawn of the rising star would prove vital in years to come. There was a particular eleven hundred mile journey on the horizon, and a strong leader would make all the difference in seeing it through.

130

Monica, safe and warm in the puppy box.

Monica, spending time out on the trapline with her dad.

Chumper in single-lead, out on the Tozi Flats.

Chapter 19

The Race Across Alaska

"Iditarod dogs in Alaska are like the Patriots in Boston."
-Stan Zuray

In the winter of 1925, a terrible epidemic of diphtheria struck the city of Nome, Alaska. With the only serum available resting nearly six hundred air miles to the southeast in Anchorage, and no way to fly in the winter, a desperate race to move the medication overland began. It traveled first by train, then was carried and passed like a baton between twenty different brave dog mushers. The serum arrived in Nome after only seven people lost their lives to the disease, which was a major victory in the face of an epidemic that threatened ten thousand lives.

In 1967, a brief, twenty five-mile memorial dog sled race was held in Alaska to commemorate the efforts of the dog mushers that carried the serum. While that competition was held, young Stan ran in a race of a different kind. His hotrod was likely pealing out, loud and proud, while various well-trained dog teams were kicking up snow.

In 1973, the very year that Stan and Charlotte landed on the Tozi River, the first ever Iditarod race was held. It ran from Anchorage to Nome, covering the entire course of the serum run, which measured about one thousand miles. The race was repeated annually from that day forward.

Now it was December 22nd, 1981. Monica was four years old, talking, walking, and maintaining strong human-dog relations on the Tozi River. Stan was downriver, visiting with Russ Wood before the holidays. A single-prop plane suddenly buzzed overhead. It was low, and getting lower. They knew they had company, stepped outside, and hiked over to the crude, gravel airstrip that Russ had created by hand. Before the plane touched the ground, they knew who the pilot was.

Clair McCann had often been enlisted to fly deliveries out to Russ and the lower Tozi gang. She taxied the plane, brought its spinner to a halt and stepped out. It was almost Christmas, and the supply run had arrived with a few extra items. Though this corner of the world would never see shiny gift-wrapping or bows, there were a few precious gifts for the homesteaders. As Russ and Stan unloaded, Clair posed a question that normally might be perceived as mere pleasantry.

"How are the dogs doing, Stan?"

"Oh they're fine." It was the same report given to Ringo after the fire took everything, and to Jack after the bear bite. Stan was just being cordial. The truth was, it was the thick of trapping season and the dogs were in pretty rough shape.

"Well, you better get into Tanana," she said. "Mike wants to talk to you. He says you're running the Iditarod."

To do a man like Mike McCann justice is a difficult thing. Most of the things he said were funny, either in the moment or five minutes later once his audience caught up with his lightning fast sense of humor. Sometimes it seemed as though for every crazy thing Stan had done, McCann had done nine. The two had a lot in common. Both grew up in cities stealing cars and making zip guns. To Stan's Boston Accent, McCann sported the sounds of Jersey, without a single complete I-N-G in his vernacular. Both loved dogs; but more than dogs, McCann loved to fly.

Unbeknownst to Stan, Mike McCann had come up with the wild idea of entering him into the thousand-mile race across Alaska. He had bought an old Cherokee 6, and was already planning on supplementing the many required costs of training and feeding dogs by flying in freight, which was a profitable racket in a place like Alaska, where roads were less common than rivers. He didn't officially have his license yet, but that didn't seem to keep the plane from getting off the ground.

It took another fifteen days for Stan to make it to town. Once he did, he tracked down the man in question to tell him just ridiculous the idea was.

"They won't have the strength, Mike. I don't have anything but Tozi salmon for them." Stan wasn't apt to complain at all, but he felt compelled to convey the very cold logic of what Mike was planning. Feeding dogs for the Iditarod wasn't a simple matter of keeping their tummies full of kibble. They needed a diet that allowed them to burn up to twelve thousand calories in one day. Without the right fat and protein, it would be like entering the Indy 500 with an empty fuel tank.

"Listen, we'll get them in shape and fill 'em up good." Mike didn't like to worry. It slowed him down too much.

"There're only seven of them, Mike." Again, Stan had a point. Most Iditarod teams were running sixteen to eighteen dogs in their teams.

"Yeah, you take good care of them, I got two here that can run with you, so that's nine."

"I don't have the money to—"

"Don't worry about the cash. I'll take care of it. I made a killing on fish eggs this year, really good money. I already paid your entry fee."

The fact that a thousand dollars had already been spent essentially sealed the deal. Stan would be running the Iditarod, no matter how under qualified and ill prepared he was.

"Small town," is a term that could have been born in Tanana. There were five hundred people in the village, and by the next day, one hundred fifty were in the know on Stan and Mike's latest scheme. Then came the beginning of not just an effort, but a movement. Stan would be the first person from Tanana to run the Iditarod. It was a landmark moment for the town, even if it was only perceived as a magnificent joke.

Over the past few years, Stan had entered his trapline team into many of the local Tanana races, all of which were sixteen mile sprints. Stan's first race had been a laughing matter for all, with a healthy portion of the laughter coming from Stan himself. He had been in town for supplies and coaxed into participating in the community event. There was never any intention of winning involved. A lightweight sled and athletic clarity would normally play key roles in the race, but Stan would ignore them on this day. He would make his run with a heavy freight sled, and although he had very little taste or skill for the art of drinking—hence the nickname "One-Can-Stan"—he had a few helpings of whiskey in his system.

He drove his team down the slip, onto the center of the wide-open, snow-covered ice of the Yukon River. Some villagers watched from high up on the riverbank, while others stayed close to the start and finish line of the looped track, intermingling with mushers, dogs, and handlers. It was springtime, and spirits were as bright as the sun.

Team after team was brought to the starting line, yelping and kicking, eager to run. Multiple handlers helped guide the teams into the chute. They untangled various lines that had been twisted in the dogs' excitement. Before the countdown was complete, most of the dogs would gleefully leap, yanking at their harnesses, craving a good sprint. It often required a few handlers, plus a buried snow hook to keep the sled from taking off prematurely.

The time came for Stan's team to line up for its shot. Without any handlers, Stan called "Gee," and "Haw." Chumper followed the directions and brought the entire team directly into the chute. The dogs halted at the starting line with an easy "whoa." Stan chuckled, waved, and enjoyed numerous bouts of banter as people patted him on the shoulder. During the remaining thirty seconds, before it was time to go, rather than the customary leaping and yelping, each of Stan's dogs laid down in the snow, closed their eyes, and tried to sleep. They had learned to get what rest they could, when they could.

"UH-kay," called Stan, and they were on their feet. Three, two, one, the starter pistol fired and the team was away. This is not a legend of Stan unexpectedly zipping around the track and taking first place, though. Quite the opposite happened on that day. Regardless of the place he took, which was very low, the event had started something. A few people took notice that, although Stan's team had been mighty slow, as they crossed the finish line they looked ready to pull for another eighteen races.

Later, Stan would return to take another race just a little more seriously, and soon prize money began to replace the income that was normally made with spring-time beaver trapping. After long winters, spending time in town for the spring races was a welcome reprieve from the trapping, skinning, and tanning of leather. Again, this was not the tale of Stan returning to clinch first place every time he ran. His speed increased, but Tanana was a place of incredibly skilled mushers. Still, the team's demeanor remained essentially the same, slow yet strong, quiet and smart.

Now, rumor had it that this trapper with a sense of humor would be entering the Iditarod. It was a contagious idea, and Stan instantly had to field a flood of support as the people of Tanana rallied behind him. Every time he journeyed to town, he seemed to take two new dogs back to the cabin with him. These were trial runs. As Stan hauled his supplies, he watched the test-dogs, checked how they ran, and determined whether or not they would pull their weight in the race. People offered a wide range of dogs, young and old. Even a few house pets made it into the mix. Stan was still a long way from having a seventeen dog team, especially with the strict vetting process that his trainees would have to make it through.

Stan went from house to house, musher to musher, getting what advice could be offered on the great race. He even left town to speak with veterans of the Iditarod.

The dogs were running greater distances and pulling heavier loads. Their calorie intake had spiked. Stan broke into his lard supply early that year, knowing that more food was on the way. The team slowly grew, ten dogs, eleven, then twelve. The influx of support allowed Stan to vet his new trainees thoroughly. He looked for good attitude, strong pullers, and intelligent dogs. Above all else, there was a narrow margin of weight that needed to be selected. If a dog was around or over sixty-five pounds, their muscle mass began to grow heavier, and their hearts shrank relative to the size. As the gap between heart size and the dog's weight grew, they slowed down accordingly. Conversely, once a dog reached the low end at forty-five pounds or less, their legs simply needed to move too fast to keep up with the others. So the constant analysis continued, into town and out, day after day.

The duration of the race would be occurring during the crucial springtime, when Stan would normally be hauling supplies out of Tanana and to his cabin before the snow melted. To make up for this, Stan had to double the frequency of his trips to town. These freight trips were the only training that his team received. On one such journey, Stan caught a message through a line of communication that was older than the telegraph: trapline chatter.

"Better get into town and talk to Mike," he was told. The words had an odd semblance to the ones Clair had spoken before, but underneath, there was one difference. They were said in a grim tone. Stan rushed into town. Once he finally reached Tanana, he received a phone call from Fairbanks with Mike McCann on the other end.

He and Clair had been stranded in Fairbanks for two days with their first load of freight. It was forty below, and a dense ice fog had settled over the airstrip. On the third day, Clair gripped the controls with white knuckles as they both made a break for it. That was when the world seemed to turn upside down. Though there was no way of understanding what had happened from within the tumbling cockpit, once they escaped the plane, it was clear. The tip of the plane's wing had caught a snow berm, knocked the plane sideways, onto its nose, and almost into a deadly somersault.

The ship was sunk. Without the income from freight hauls, they wouldn't have the funding to feed the dogs, or buy the gear that Stan needed to compete in the race. Two days later, Mike returned to Tanana via commercial bush flight, and offered Stan the only two bags of dog food he could manage. That night they sat, calculated, and debated. The remaining fish that Stan had were as flat as pancakes and low in nutrients. The lack of fat and protein was miles beyond a minor issue. As for gear, the dogs still needed booties to protect their feet. This was no minor purchase, as over the course of one thousand miles, most would be lost and some would be worn down. On top everything, there was no way for Stan and his team to get to the starting line in Anchorage. The discussion concluded with one crucial sentiment.

"We've never needed money before."

It was true. The two of them were a can-do duo. Previously, they had teamed up in bringing an upside down, long deceased plane out of the woods and thirty miles down the Yukon River for repairs. It was eventually restored, and returned to the sky. There was some kind of synergy between the two of them. They agreed to continue the endeavor, no matter how hopeless it seemed.

Once again, the people of Tanana threw their weight behind the team. They held a pancake breakfast in town, fundraising to cover some of the costs. People were no longer simply offering dogs, but food as well. Somewhere along the line, Stan's entry into the race started being taken more seriously. Within these times, Stan's Iditarod name was born, and he would often be referred to as, "Hip Hip Zuray."

The money that was raised went towards booties for the dogs. They wouldn't have enough to be worn throughout training as they should, but their feet would be protected for the race itself.

Come race time, the Iditarod Airforce—a varied collection of planes and volunteer bush pilots—would be making supply drops for the mushers at every checkpoint. At roughly two bags per stop, this meant Stan and Mike would have to create roughly fifty sacks full of fresh socks for Stan, booties for the dogs, and food for all. Slowly, the two began gathering better, stronger food. They were invited to stay as guests at a house in Fairbanks, and as the time of the race drew near, they flew into town to package and ship the bulk of the food. Stan got hold of a sheet of plywood, which he covered in plastic and set up as a table in the home's backyard. He and McCann mixed together clumps of beef, chicken, and liver with a dash of vitamins. The mixture was divided, formed into patties, and left outside on the plywood table to freeze overnight.

The time came to get moving. With no roads leading into Tanana, Stan would be driving his team to Nenana, roughly one-hundred and twenty miles away, where their ride to Anchorage was waiting. Within the first twenty-five miles of the journey, the dogs suddenly commenced vomiting all over the snow. The night before, Stan had broken into the first of his high-protein food patties and the dogs simply weren't used to the food. Fortunately, a dog vomiting meant something different than a human performing the same act. Back in the lineage, mother wolves often ate and regurgitated meals for their pups. In essence, the dogs weren't sick, they were throwing up to keep from getting sick.

The trail to Nenana was just a touch cold, and the traveling took only three days. As Stan pulled up, there sat Mike McCann, and an old 1963 International Pickup. A large dog box sat on top of the truck bed, with individual homes for each of the dogs to keep them out of each other's business.

John Hewitt hopped out of the driver's seat, and greeted Stan with an eager handshake. This was the man that had once helped Stan double his accuracy with a rifle. Now he would be driving the homesteader right up to the starting line of the Iditarod. They set to work and one by one, scrambling and barking, the dogs were loaded into their respective boxes.

The road out of Nenana was rough, with a steep embankment waiting on either side. One of McCann's idiosyncrasies came out along that road. Even though he had no problem flying planes through wind and storms, he couldn't stand a dangerous ride in an old truck. McCann had only started to suggest that John slow his roll, when the front driver-side tire exploded.

The truck swerved harsh to the left, juked right, and then back to the left and straight towards the embankment. McCann held the passenger side door half open; ready to make a jump for it if things got any worse. The remaining tires grinded against the dirt road and brought the truck to a stop along with all twenty of the life forms on board.

There was only a collective sigh before the gang hopped out and put on their pit crew hats. As they worked, Stan commented on how lucky they had been that the dog box was bolted down to the truck. With all the tossing and turning, the thing might have flown right off and taken each of the dogs for a ride down the embankment. John gave his head a scratch.

"You know, I was going to get to that but we just didn't seem to have time for it."

Three pairs of wide eyes showed on the outside, while inside, each man in his own way thought the same basic sentiment: "Thank God."

The tire went on first. Then came the straps. Up and over they were tossed, then tied down. Ideally, securing the dog box would have been done with hardware instead of straps, but the whole experience thus far had operated at levels just below ideal. No need to change now. So the journey to Anchorage continued, with three lucky men, seventeen luckier dogs, and an old noisy truck half held together by straps.

The roads grew wider and began to smooth out, the hours ticked by, and soon came Anchorage. This would be the location of the race's ceremonial start. The trio and their furry groupies pulled into a lot that was full of new trucks that had been cleaned up for the big day. As team "Hip-hip Zuray's" twenty-year old ride squeaked to a halt, the only thing missing from the scene was a backfire, busting its way out of the tailpipe.

First on the agenda was a visit to the Iditarod veterinarian. Humane treatment of each musher's living, breathing engine was something that the race took very seriously. Keeping close watch over the dogs at every checkpoint, as well as flying in their food was no small operation. Mike's payment of the one thousand dollar entry fee had not been for profit.

At the vet's office, Stan's race almost concluded before it began.

He was only able to afford protective boots for the race itself, not the training. The dog's paws were in rough shape, and each had various cuts and breaks on their pads.

It was somewhat common for one or two of a musher's dogs to be put on notice throughout the race. Breaking the norm, Stan's entire team was put on notice before the race even began. He wasn't disqualified, but from the first checkpoint forward, the vets would be watching the tiny paws closer, making sure their condition didn't deteriorate.

Lastly, the vets put stethoscopes to fur and checked each dog's heart. All was fine until Chumper. The loyal, intelligent dog seemed to have an oddly accelerated and shallow heart beat. It was bizarre, and so uncommon that the vets had no idea how serious the anomaly actually was. To be safe, they would pull Chumper from the race.

Stan leapt to his defense. This was no weak dog with a troubled heart. In fact, there had been no signs of trouble at all. Chumper had been pulling harder than the rest of his team. He was the leader, he was the strongest, and removing him would be catastrophic. Stan told them all of this. In the end, evidence of good health won out over the unknown condition, and Chumper remained in the team.

Stan awoke the next morning feeling as though he hadn't slept at all. This might have had something to do with the fact that he and his friends didn't have a place to spend the night, and opted to pull off to the side of the road and sleep in the truck.

Since sled dogs were often skittish and apt to distraction, the pomp, circumstance, photos and cheering was all done prior to the race, at a ceremonial start. After Stan's moment of fame at Chumper's side and in front of cameras, it was time for the three men to pile into their truck and join the parade out of Anchorage, clearly driving the eldest of all the vehicles by a margin of twenty years.

Halfway up the last hill out of town, a traffic light turned red, and the parade came to a stop. The truck's brakes were bad and the transmission was loose. Stopping on an incline was not recommended, but they were pinned in the procession. A full crowd of eyes and cameras were watching. Slowly at first, the truck started to roll backwards. In his rear view mirror, John Hewitt could see a look of terror on the driver behind him. He repeatedly pumped the brakes, but the truck's roll continued. Stan slid over from his middle seat and joined in the downward mash on the brake system, freeing up John to make fancy footwork out of the clutch. All the way down, there was McCann, hand on the door handle, ready to bail.

The truck stopped within one foot of its back neighbor, the light turned a merciful green, and the gang made it up over the hill and out of town. It was the last major obstacle to occur before the beginning of the race, and a mere ant mound compared to the mountains that lay still ahead for Stan.

A slow ride, a quick sleep in the truck, a rapid unload, and a long wait later, Stan was in line for the start. He had drawn poorly for his starting position, and would have to wait for the thirty teams ahead of him to get under way. The difference in time would be accounted for later, but it didn't make the waiting any easier.

Finally, the dogs were in the chute, and Stan was ready for blast off. Iditarod dog handlers buzzed around his team, untangling lines and untwisting harness straps. Over the PA system, the announcer hassled Stan over his attire. Most mushers glided up to the line in a proper parka and snow pants. Stan's snow pants were old as sin, and had actually been cut out of a pair of coveralls. On top of that, he was only wearing a sweater. It was still a nice day as far as he was concerned.

The announcer gave a thirty-second warning. Stan looked down to all of his gear. The race required that he bring a sleeping bag, axe, snowshoes, boots for the dogs, and a starter poundage of food. Also thrown into the mix was a bag of mail, symbolic of the struggle of old postal workers before the advent of aviation. Common, but not required in those days, was a two-burner Coleman stove that had been chopped down to one. Though single burners were available in plenty, the sheer volume of water and food that needed preparing also required a stove with a wide, strong base. It was a unique way to save both weight and cooking time.

The sled also had a machete for quick preparation of spruce beds for the dogs, an ice scraper for the runners, and a brush to remove snow from outer clothing layers before it melted into a problem.

The announcer started his ten-second countdown.

Nine seconds.

On the sidelines, McCann and John Hewitt were going ballistic. It was mostly due to excitement for what Stan was about to undertake, but also in part because they had actually made it to this point without the wheels falling off.

Five seconds.

Stan thought about all the work that had led to this moment. Many mushers prepare for this race over the course of the entire year, with thirty to one hundred thousand dollars in sponsorship at their backs. Considering Stan had only four thousand dollars and three months to train, it was amazing that he was even standing at the starting line today. The miracle was entirely thanks to the people of Tanana. After a life of running from people, Stan had finally been embraced by a community that he both loved and respected. The past three months had brought a new meaning to the phrase, "It takes a village."

Four.

By this year, the typical start-to-finish time of the race was twelve days. The Iditarod Airforce had gotten more sophisticated, the volunteer base had grown, and the gear had improved a great deal since the times of twenty-day races. This year, however, storms would interfere. Fighting the snow and blow, the first mushers would not be crossing the finish line until sixteen days after their start, while the slowest mushers would have to endure twenty-six days on the trail. It would remain among the longest, toughest races in Iditarod history.

Three, Two, One...

Mike McCann (left) and Stan (right) inside of the abandoned plane that needed just a little work.

John's 1963 International Harvester. New dog boxes, no brakes.

From Left: Mike McCann, Stan, and Clair McCann at the ceremonial start, in Anchorage.

At the starting line, ready for lift off.

Chapter 20
Northward, to Nome

The first forty-two miles hadn't gone well. Stan's position had dropped from fortieth to forty-sixth. He hadn't let his spirits deflate much with each passing dog team, though, as he wasn't operating at full speed yet. There were a lot of kinks to work out. The sled was heavy and the few breaks he had taken were slow to end. Now, it was after dark at Yetna, the very first checkpoint of the race. Some of the lead mushers had already taken a six-hour rest and pressed on to Skwentna, which sat an additional thirty miles away.

Traveling at night was common during the early, southern lengths of the Iditarod when the weather was warmer. It looked as though tonight Stan's six-hour break would take him close to sunrise. With the dogs tied up, Stan crossed the way through the dark and unfamiliar town, towards the lights of the checkpoint's namesake lodge. Inside they had water, which was actually a courtesy. More often than not, mushers would be melting their water out of snow. The lodge had also received Stan's very first shipment of food, dry socks, and dog boots that he had packaged a few weeks prior.

Outside the lodge, Stan encountered one particularly large musher. They talked about the first forty-two miles, and in a moment, the musher rolled a joint and offered it to Stan. Suddenly, Stan's entire perception of the race was thrown for a loop. Months back, after his conversation with Mike McCann, he had sworn off even beer, because he wanted to be in peak condition.

Now, here was a man ready to smoke some dope and relax. Was this what the race was about? Was it a collection of easy-going folks just looking to get high and have a nice ride? He simply had no cultural reference or compass to steer by. After some frazzled thoughts, Stan declined, assuming that this man was the exception, not the norm.

Walking back to his dogs, perhaps feeling just a touch lonely, he readied himself for a night beneath the stars. He pulled out his cable gang line, adorned it with eighteen heavy chains, and strung it up between trees. Next, he pulled his dogs from their harnesses, and hooked them onto their respective chains. After hanging the harness for a little airing out, Stan rolled out his tarp, then sleeping mat, then sleeping bag, and finally crashed into sleep.

The sun was suddenly up, and there was movement all around him. Stan awoke to see that it was time to get moving, once again. Though he couldn't tell in the previous night's darkness, he could now see it perfectly clear: he had made a mistake. The musher beside him popped up from his bag, which had been resting inside his sled, thus eliminating the need for a sleeping pad. Not one dog in sight had been de-harnessed and chained to a gang line. Instead, they had all slept the entire night through in their running positions. Within two minutes of waking up, Stan's neighboring dog musher was on his sled, and calling "Let's go! Let's go!" The team slid off, rejoining the race.

Stan scrambled. It was all he could do. He ran between gang line and sled, harnessing dogs one at a time. He rolled up his pad and tucked away his bag. Fifteen minutes later, he was ready to go, with one exception. The gang line remained stretched between two trees just thirty feet away. Stan regarded it only for a moment. It was the heaviest thing in his sled, and it was now useless.

"UH-kay!" he commanded, and the dogs took off. It's difficult to say how long the giant paperweight dangled there, but Stan never saw it again.

The traveling that day involved a great deal of open country. Stan was already admitting to himself that he was out of the race, and starting to feel like a punch line that he couldn't quite laugh at. The race was starting to sort itself out now. Original starting positions began to jumble, and spread into racing positions. The slow teams were falling behind, and the future winners were making their way towards the front. Stan was definitively a part of the former group.

His next six-hour rest, at the Skwentna checkpoint, was largely spent examining veteran mushers, and taking tips from anyone who had them. Later, Stan returned to his sled for another night of sleeping in the mild chill of southern Alaska. It would be the last time in the race that he and his competitors would be traveling without a massive storm system trying to stop them.

The trail to Finger Lake brought him another forty miles closer to Nome. He drew nearer to the mountains and slowly started his climb into the high country. As his team pulled upward, the beginnings of snowfall arrived. To keep the dogs going strong, Stan consistently rested them for five minutes every hour, and fifteen for every three. During each of these breaks, he gave the panting canines pats and rubs of encouragement. The dogs were, as of yet, his only trail companions.

By the time he reached Finger Lake, Stan was eight hours behind the leading pack, which was mighty discouraging considering this was only the first one-hundred and twenty mile stretch, and he would be an additional six behind once his mandatory rest concluded. Regardless of demoralizing thoughts, Stan was able to enjoy good food inside, sitting at a table with some of the other mushers. The socializing was nice, and the talk was all the same: people were beginning to catch word that the weather ahead was evolving into something ugly.

Always thinking ahead, Stan was of two minds on the storm. The snow might slow down the leaders of the pack, and grant him a chance to close the gap between their teams and his. On the other hand, a gossip-worthy blizzard was of great concern. The leaders had traveled this trail before. Stan had not. If he strayed from the trail, he would pay dearly for it.

One rest later, the trails to the checkpoint at Rainy Pass, and then to Rohn were as bad as the weather. There were long, slippery, glaciered downhill stretches where control was greatly reduced. Stan traversed narrow, frozen creeks that had been covered with sloshy, watery overflow. In the narrowest points of the creek, the sled bounced and smacked from one bank to the other, and Stan began to feel his ride falling to pieces. He was getting far up into the mountains now, and was more alone than all previous stretches. Whereas before he would have to occasionally pull over to let an advancing team pass, this time there was truly no one. The team climbed, higher and higher into the mountains. The snow was thick enough to obstruct most of the view. Along the race, he would travel through the Alaska Mountain Range and through countless incredible landscapes, but the snow would keep him from seeing any of it.

Next thing Stan knew, after a bruising and battering along the trail, he somehow started passing other teams. It wasn't many, but enough to lift his spirits. Though he had not the slightest idea what position he had advanced to, it was clear that something was happening. Teams had been bedding down more often, thanks to the weather.

At one point along the race, all mushers were required to take one twenty-four hour rest at the checkpoint of their choosing. This meant there was a stretch of three or four checkpoints along the way that each musher had sent a double ration of food in order to keep their options open. Once Stan dragged into Rohn on his broken sled, some of the mushers had already started their twenty-four hours. Stan didn't have the benefit of options, though, as the only double-drop he could afford was another two checkpoints—one hundred and twenty miles—away, in McGrath. As the race went on, Stan would garner the reputation of being the musher that shipped the least poundage into each checkpoint.

Stan briefly considered taking his twenty-four hour rest in Rohn, even though he didn't have the food to sustain such a break. His sled was in pieces and the lack of sleep was catching up with him. He had already stopped considering the race a competition. By now, the Iditarod was just a long ride.

All hopes of an extended stay at Rohn vanished when Stan stopped in to collect his food. There was none. Rohn was a difficult landing for bush planes regardless of weather, and the storm had made it next to impossible. Some mushers had been lucky enough to see their food land, but Stan wasn't one of them.

So it was another six hours of rest, at least for the dogs. Stan spent four of those hours repairing his ruined sled. He tied it together with rope and straps, following the fashion theme of the truck that had gotten him into the mess in the first place. He pulled up the runners and tied a few knots, recreating their bend at the sled's front, so they would quit plowing the snow.

Some of the locals offered Stan a pack of hotdogs. If he was going to miss all of his sleep, they hoped he could at least fill his stomach during his stay. Stan thanked them and accepted the offering. To be polite, he pretended that he was going off to have a private feast; instead, he broke the hot dogs in two and gave one portion to each dog in his team.

During his stay, Stan managed to surprise the veterinarians a great deal. Despite running seventy miles per day, his team's paws had actually healed since leaving Anchorage. So went the proof that dog boots truly worked. Of all the things working against him, at least Stan knew he wouldn't be disqualified any time soon. The dogs had been holding up great, especially considering the conditions.

Stan, now thinking ahead and beyond the race, realized that regardless of whether he finished the race or not, he would be returning to normal life afterward. He would need a new litter of pups come summer. Chumper had been performing fantastically. Sweeper, a blonde-furred and particularly chipper female, had also been pulling way more than her weight, and good genes were sometimes hard to come by. So, while Stan was making repairs to his sled, he let Chumper and Sweeper loose, hoping they would enjoy a little tryst. Chumper made his move, and six people all around perked up, yelled varying degrees of "whoa!" and charged towards the mating dogs, trying to break them up.

Stan informed them that everything was fine, it was all according to plan. The other mushers, some of them the veterans that were leading the race, questioned how anything could possibly be fine about two dogs breeding on the Iditarod trail. It was difficult to convince the group that there was any sense to be found in the dogs being allowed to hump, but eventually the crowd dispersed, heads shaking in disapproval.

Somewhere in that blur of sleepless, hungry, bush mechanic work, Stan was given a crucial tip off on his status in the race. Twenty-two of the participants in that year's race were rookies. As far as novice racers were concerned, Stan was one of three mushers in sight of the "Rookie of the Year," award. This spun Stan's mindset up into a whole new direction. For the first time since the race had started, he felt as though he was really competing for something.

The six-hour mark of his stay in Rohn was approaching. Having not so much as rolled out his sleeping bag all night, Stan had planned on staying a couple of extra hours beyond the six for some desperately needed sleep. Previous distances between checkpoints were topping off at only forty miles, but the run from here to the next stop was seventy-five. Sleep was even more essential at this point, because Stan's twenty-four hour break was still a long ways off. Now, though, he had something to run for. Rookie of the Year was, perhaps, within his grasp. Without a wink of sleep at his back, Stan set off for checkpoint Nikolai.

He found it was the first checkpoint to remind him of home. Rather than a vacation lodge, or a massive house in the woods, Nikolai was a native Athabascan village on the Kuskokwim River drainage. He was greeted first by children. They rushed up to him in search of autographs and a chance to pet the tired dogs. Next, he was approached by residents that had been told by their Tanana relatives to keep an eye out for him. Slowly, Stan remembered that he wasn't in the race alone. There was an entire village pushing him from behind.

Even the ride between checkpoints had been friendlier. Stan had joined a group of ten mushers that agreed to travel together. Though there was plenty of leap-frogging for the lead within the gang, most agreed to stop and enjoy their breaks together.

While in Nikolai, Stan found himself thinking that it was good to be home, though Tanana was far away. Unfortunately, the visit would be short-lived. His double food drop was still forty-eight miles away. Even though most of the mushers in town would be staying here for twenty-four hours, Stan would be leaving after only six.

Perseverance Furthers.

By virtue of this hiccup in his planning, Stan achieved something that he never thought possible. That night, while the rest of the teams were either just arriving, or resting, Stan got under way, and his position officially moved up. He was now in first place.

He made sure to enjoy the victorious feeling and empty trail while it lasted. He knew that once he arrived in McGrath, his extended layover would cost him way more than just the first position. His place was merely an illusion caused by the rotation of rest periods, though it was still a very nice illusion.

What he hadn't anticipated, though, was that McGrath would be an overwhelming bustle of activity. It was a larger town, and one of the few major airplane hubs of Alaska. The village had filled up with news reporters and spectators. Stan, who had slept about twenty-five hours total in the past week, was quickly pulled aside for a television interview.

"What's the hardest part of the Iditarod?" went the question.

Stan told her all about what, to him, was completely obvious. The blurry eyes and trembles of sleep deprivation were wreaking havoc on him. The reporter changed her tone, turning the interview into more of a conversation. She spoke of many mushers struggling with a lack of sleep. Often, they would even hallucinate on the trail. Stan let her know that the hallucinations didn't bother him; he had done a lot of LSD as a kid and was pretty accustomed to seeing things that weren't there. The entire interview made air.

Finally, after another long haul, came the coveted rest that Stan so craved, though he didn't spend the entire time resting. His sled, keeping up with its motif, was in complete shambles. A friend of Stan's had put a great deal of work into crafting the ride, and it had been an impressive view from the outside. Within, however, no one knew that the wrong variety of glue had been used, and it was failing. Stan once again took to shoring up his ride. He didn't care about weight or efficiency anymore. All he wanted was to stop spending his layover periods tying knots. He got hold of some heavy, black, iron water pipes and began securing them to his battered transport. They were heavier than the moon, but at least he knew they would keep everything in one piece.

The sled was sturdy, but the racing operation as a whole still seemed ready to fall apart. After his twenty-four hours, Stan had lost so much of his lead that it felt like the bad-old days of Yentna and Rohn. The dogs didn't spring to their feet at the first sound of Stan's voice that morning. They were wearing down.

Just out of McGrath, on the way to Takotna, another crucial linchpin in the operation started to bend. Chumper was limping. He was still pulling with everything he had, but "everything" seemed now to only include three legs. Stan called "Whoa," brought the team to a stop, and checked on his gifted lead dog. Chumper panted, tongue out, surveying his snowy surroundings while Stan dove into their unscheduled doctor's appointment. The paw in question looked worked, but not enough to cause a limp. This left only one possibility: Chumper had pulled a muscle.

By this point in the race, one-fourth of the team had stopped pulling their lines tight. This effect was cascading, as the slacked straps on some dogs meant more work for the rest. Stan pulled young Chumper from the lead and placed him in the sled for a little ride. This meant that not only was the team losing one of its stronger pullers, it was gaining an extra fifty-eight pounds of cargo.

Days blew by, through snow and wind. The team made it to Takotna, then Ophir. All the while, Stan and the dogs were taking a beating from the strong gusts. Every single time that Stan stopped along the way, out came the machete. He meticulously assembled extra-comfortable spruce bough beds for each dog, and rested them for as long as possible. Chumper was alternated in and out of the team. Likewise, his limp appeared and disappeared over the course of the next one hundred miles.

Finally, Stan and his team pulled into an appropriately named checkpoint known only as "Cripple." With that, another low point set in. The sled simply wasn't going to make it to the end of the race. All of the duct tape, cord, chain, and welding in the world couldn't save it. The previous lengths between checkpoints had gotten much longer, and as a result, Stan had run out of dog boots. The paws of each dog were starting to look ugly.

Despite his best efforts brushing away powder, Stan's winter-wear had gotten too wet to dry during his rests. Considering the state of his gear and dogs, one might think that this was the home stretch. Maybe, if they got one final burst of energy, they could drag Stan, surfing a fragment of his sled, across the finish line. This wasn't the case.

Hip-Hip Zuray and his dogs had only made it halfway into the race. With another five hundred miles ahead of them, winning Rookie of the Year was rendered impossible, and the prospect of even finishing the race was under heavy scrutiny.

Forced to press on and make it to his twenty-four hour rest in McGrath, Stan enjoys a quick soda before leaving Nikolai. He was in first place when he left this village.

Fitting a homemade canvas boot onto Chumper.

Chapter 21

Angels and Allies

As Stan approached the village of Ruby, spectators began to crop up in increasing numbers. Snow machines were pulled off to the side of the road. People cheered and held signs. Some of the signs, to Stan's surprise, read "Hip-hip Zuray!" His friends from Tanana had traveled downriver; many of them making a one hundred mile journey overland through the same snow and wind just to be there.

As the dogs dragged Stan's giant snow shovel into town, Stan called "Whoa!" and the whole operation grinded to a stop, right at the feet of Stan's guardian angel. Mike McCann had gotten his old Cherokee flying again, and rode the wind in to pay Stan a visit. He was wearing his usual tricky, worry-free grin.

The team and sled were moved to their resting place, and the dogs dropped into sleep almost instantly. Stan and McCann stood over the pile of sticks and iron pipe, trying to figure out if there was a way to un-toast bread. This was when McCann sent Stan to bed. Stan put up about as much fight over the matter as someone could when they were capable of sleeping standing up. In the end, he agreed to only a couple hours, and McCann claimed the sled problem as his own.

That night, Stan dreamed of more snow and wind. Even in his slumber, he was given no quarter. McCann pulled him out of one dream and into another four hours later. He was invited outside to take a look at the makeover that had been given to his battered ride. As Stan stepped out into the snow, he saw not just another repair job, but an entirely new sled. The brand-new basket sled was a combination of beautiful woodwork and functionality. Stan, imagining a heavenly ray of light from above, stepped onto the sled's runners and gripped its curved wooden handles. He rocked left, he rocked right, and he could have hugged McCann. The thing was a new dream, all of its own.

While Stan was sleeping, McCann had hit the ground running in search of a solution. After some quick detective work, he found a Ruby local and Iditarod veteran that had just ordered a new sled from Fairbanks. It had been broken down into pieces to fit on the plane, but it was here. McCann told the local musher all about Stan's situation, and even showed him the old bucket of problems. The musher agreed to loan out the sled, and McCann swore to return it to him once the race was over. For the remaining hours, before waking Stan, McCann and the musher had worked away at constructing the sled, and completed it just in time for the end of Stan's official rest period.

After some goodbyes with his Tanana cheering squad and the guardian angel himself, Stan glided off, back into the race. He dropped down the riverbank, onto the old familiar Yukon River. This intersection would be the closest he came to home for the length of the entire race. Up river, to his right, sat Tanana, The Site, and the mouth of the Tozitna River. Left, and downriver, was the remainder of the race. Stan turned left.

The difference in speed was far beyond noticeable, and one other small miracle had seemingly occurred over night. Chumper's limp disappeared. The dog healed himself over the course of a one-hundred and eighty mile run, and would continue running on all four legs for the rest of the race.

Galena, then Nulato, then Kaltag. The one hundred and thirty miles were easier in some ways and harder in others. Speed, efficiency, and spirits had all improved along the way. On the other hand, the seemingly endless bends of the river blurred together and grew monotonous. Riding through the Yukon River valley brought temperatures into a nosedive. The cold was quickly mitigated by the accommodations in Kaltag. The town had opted to assign hosts and homes to each musher, and Stan was given a warm bed and quiet house for the night.

Before sleep that evening, Stan started a friendship that would continue long after the Iditarod's conclusion. Don Honea had run the great race four times prior to meeting Stan. Though he couldn't quite be called an "old timer," he had just enough years on Stan to become a sort of Iditarod father figure. The two of them got to talking, and immediately found that their laid-back personas meshed well. They left Kaltag within minutes of each other, and quickly switched from competitors to teammates. It was an alliance that proved to be vital in the face of what was waiting for them.

On the way to Unalakleet (pronounced Yuna-Kleet by the entire population of Alaska), more of the all-too-common snow and blow did its best to stop the men. They were in the top twenty now, which was encouraging, and if they managed to maintain that, they would at least earn one of the twenty cash prizes that were waiting at the finish line. Unfortunately, the trail left by the leaders was hidden under a deep powdery snowdrift. Between them and the large group ahead, there was a storm doing its best to conceal the trail entirely.

In places, the duo had to step off of their sleds and wade into the powder without snowshoes, as it was the only way they could detect the trail beneath. Stan was able to redirect this team with ease, thanks to Chumper at the lead. Often with leaders, the commands "Gee," and "Haw," yielded ambiguous changes in direction. Chumper, though, was laser accurate; and depending on intensity and repetition of the call, could navigate around the exact tree that Stan had in mind.

A dichotomy began to form between Stan and Don. In deep, trail-less snow, Stan's team often did the better of the two. On hard trail, however, Don's team proved faster. In difficult conditions, the two mushers stuck close and worked as a team. Whenever things smoothed out, there would often be some distance between them, but the leader would always stop to ensure the follower was close behind.

As they pulled into Unalakleet that day, Don informed Stan that he was on a first name basis with a few of the locals. Though no houses were assigned to mushers at this stop, Don invited Stan to stay with some friends, and for the second night in a row, he had a warm bed to sleep in. That night, outside, the storm reached a new level of intensity. The gusts were powerful enough to lay fifteen-foot drift piles up against most of the homes. Even more shocking than that, the streets had been blown down to bare ground. Though the weather would die down before their departure the next day, the previous night was a good example of what they would be running into outside of their next checkpoint at Shaktoolik.

The crew expanded when two other mushers joined them, and the four traveled in a loose pack through hills and flurries, away from

Unalakleet. Once they dropped down in elevation, they were met by the incredible winds of the Alaskan West Coast. The air had kicked into high gear just as the sun was setting.

Stan could barely see his lead dogs, and even the snow beneath him had turned into an ambiguous wind-swept cloud. The game of stop-and-go reached an all-new level. Stan was yet again off of his sled and stomping around in the powder, trying to satisfy his craving for some hard-pack. Every time he did this, he had to tip his sled onto its side, so as not to catch the brunt of a strong gust. Once his feet struck the trail, he tipped his sled back upward and led onward. No sooner, a gust of wind smacked the broad side of Stan's sled like a car, and sent it swinging ninety degrees out from Chumper's intended direction, nearly throwing Stan from the sled. He recovered, and moved the team back into alignment.

The storm did not let up, and eventually the four mushers gathered to yell their plan over the wind. The conditions were such that no one could be left behind. They would stay as close as possible, and each member of the line would look out for the one behind him.

As it turned out, one would be left behind anyway, but not by mistake. Stan turned to see the man waving his hands, and called, "Whoa!" The dogs not only stopped, but dropped. They were ducking under the wind. If not for this move, they would be blown over.

The musher behind Stan put it simply. "I quit."

Rather than press on through the mess, he wanted to hunker down and wait for the storm to pass. It was a decision made not just for himself, but his dogs. Their strength was just about used up. Stan and the others helped the musher get settled; turning his sled into a shelter. The crew was now down to three.

Even Chumper was starting to waver. His strength and intelligence was impressive, but the situation boiled down to a need for age and experience. Just a couple of positions back, still pulling her hardest, was Grizzly. If dogs can feel pride, Grizzly was probably full of it for the majority of the race. She was Chumper's mother, and had likely been responsible for his strong genes.

The situation was iced over and dire. Stan knew that keeping the dogs calm was the new highest priority. The only way to get them through conditions like these was to make them think that everything was ok—which it most certainly was not. Every time he stopped, he would go down the line, giving his dogs a comforting rub, and speaking soft words of encouragement.

On more than one occasion, he noticed the team was missing the trail even when markers were visible. He made another pass of encouragement only to find that most of the dog's eyes had been iced shut. They were running blind, based entirely on Stan's various "Gees" and "Haws." He delicately rubbed each of their eyes open, pretending not to notice the wind.

Now, the third musher began losing his wits. He passed Don, who had previously been in the middle, caught up to Stan, and decided to yell at him. He couldn't understand what the deal was with all of the stopping. He knew the only way for them to get out of this was to keep going. He was sure of it.

Stan asked him to lower his voice. If he upset the dogs, he would sink the ship. If they wanted to travel on trail, they had to take it slow. At this point, even if the musher spooked his own dogs, the fear would be contagious, and have disastrous effects on the rest of the convoy. Stan encouraged the musher to stay behind him. He knew his own dogs could make it through conditions just like these, and Don agreed. With just about nothing resolved, musher number three huffed, and returned to his team. Ten minutes later, Stan heard him screaming at the top of his lungs from behind, driving his dogs like slaves.

The musher shouted louder and larger than any of them had done through the entire thick of the storm. He drove his team into the powder, and slowly passed Stan. The moment was reminiscent of Cleetsa's mad desire to take the lead.

Positions and speed meant absolutely nothing at this point, and Stan decided to hang back and let a new musher take on the burden of leading. The ambitious leader's dogs lost the trail within an eighth of a mile, charged into powder, and collapsed into a tangled ball. Both Stan and Don helped him get his line straight, then urged him to hang back and allow his team to follow one of them. The musher agreed to do one further. He would stay put for the remainder of the storm, even if it took two days to blow over.

Once again, Stan and Don got their teammate settled, said their goodbyes, and the gang was reduced to its original two. Life went on that same way for hours. It seemed they were trapped in some kind of infinity loop of cold darkness. There was not a single sign of civilization until—

All at once, both men saw a small, wooden fish rack. A little further up, and there were smoke houses. Both considered pulling over and spending the night in one of the shacks, but they knew the checkpoint must be close by. They were right; and as the two pulled into the town, their struggle against the winds of Shaktoolik drew to a close. They soon found out that there were only eight other teams resting at the checkpoint. Among the waylaid mushers was the leading rookie that Stan had been chasing since Rohn. As Stan and Don made the rounds at the checkpoint, they realized that they were in good company. Both had made it to the top ten.

The storm had been so bad and so large that no teams had left Unalakleet after Stan and Don's departure. From Shaktoolik, only one of the leaders had attempted to leave in a daring try for the next checkpoint, at Koyuk. Herbie Nayokpuk was an exceptionally experienced musher of Eskimo descent that had earned top ten placings six of the eight times that he had run the race. He had hoped to use the weather as his chance to get ahead of the rest of the teams. Stan and Don wouldn't learn this until later, but the weather somehow managed to bring Herbie to a halt only twenty miles outside of Shaktoolik. He spent the night in his sled, and was forced to turn around the next morning for the sake of his battered team.

Other than Herbie's endeavor, and the slower racers that were piling up at Unalakleet, the race remained at a standstill for two days. The first morning, Stan stepped outside to check on his dogs. He had found the perfect spot behind a large oil tank that would shield them from the wind. When he arrived, however, he found nothing but snow.

"UH-kay!" he called. Heads and wagging tails burst upward through the snowdrift. The dogs actually seemed happy, as if they had just enjoyed the best sleep of the entire race. The snow that covered them while they slept had made a terrific shelter, and kept them warm through the night. They quickly engaged in a prolonged shaking ritual, sending droplets and clumps of snow in all directions.

All nine teams were stuck in Shaktoolik for two full days. What followed was utterly surreal, compared to prior stretches of the trip. During this time, Stan was able to enjoy a few bouts of basketball in the town's high school gymnasium. He couldn't dribble or shoot any better than he could fly, but just like those original Tanana races, he turned his inexperience into a comedy show. He spent the majority of the game double dribbling and entertaining what spectators he had.

On the third day, as the weather began to lift, Stan and Don caught word that the leaders had started making their departures. They went to their teams, woke up their dogs, and drove to the checkpoint's starting line. The miles ticked by from there, fifty miles to Koyuk, forty-eight to Elim, and another twenty-eight to Golovin. The dogs were, understandably, getting stubborn now. Sometimes, at the day's start, Stan would have to walk over to them, lift them onto their feet, and brush the snow off of their fur for them. Much of the team had stopped pulling entirely. Their lines were slack and they were quite simply along for the ride.

Rather than drive them hard, Stan kept a constant, soft song of encouragement going, turning his voice hoarse. He whistled and called out, "You good dogs."

He conversed with them as if they could talk back.

Every twenty miles or so, the dogs would come to a stop. Stan would interrupt his song with a quick raspy shout. "COME ON, COME ON, LET'S GO!" The dogs would resume their trot, and Stan would return to his chanting and whistling.

The weather was still less than ideal, but gallons better than it had been outside of Shaktoolik. The improved conditions allowed Stan and Don to leave space between one another, though they continued to leapfrog each other all the way to White Mountain.

On the way into the checkpoint, while Stan was leading Don, he saw a distant team ahead. It was small, like a black bead on a white tablecloth. The bead grew, and soon Stan recognized the sled and the call its driver was chanting. Stan was looking at Dean Osmar, the leading rookie of the race. His style had been one of a hard-driving sprinter. It had served him well for the first nine hundred miles of the race, and allowed him to enjoy a great deal of time spent among the leaders. Now, though, his team was tired and shrinking in numbers. As Stan gained ground, Dean politely pulled to the side of the trail, not stopping, but allowing Stan room to pass. As he did, they made their cordial "hellos," and "goodbyes." It was another unbelievable milestone in the journey. Stan was now lined up for Rookie of the Year.

The checkpoint at White Mountain looked exactly as Stan

suspected it would, snow-covered and mountainous. Time was moving faster now, and though the mandatory rest was eight hours long, it seemed to be over in a blink. Just like that, he was waking up in his sled once again. The motions had become fully automatic by now. Stan mounted his sled and called out to his team. The only checkpoint between him and Nome was an optional stay at Safety. He and Don had only seventy miles to go. There would be no more six-hour rests now, and the time for the final push had come.

Tanana residents cheering Stan on, outside of Ruby.

Carl Minetti assembling Stan's new Iditarod sled at Ruby. Photo taken by Mike McCann on one of his rare breaks.

Making ready to depart Kaltag.

Chapter 22
The Burled Arch

Susan Butcher and Rick Swenson were career dog mushers. Between the two of them, they had run the great race nearly ten times, and always placed well, thanks to strong teams and stronger experience. Now, on the final stretch of the Iditarod, Don and Stan were ahead of them.

It meant very little, of course. Like in Nikolai, the position was a mere anomaly, produced by staggered rest periods. Regardless of cause, effect, or outcome, it felt pretty good to have nothing but snow between Chumper's nose, and Nome.

During Stan and Don's next rest, as they were enjoying a quick trailside snack, they saw the seven leaders approaching. Stan, in his typical young and eager fashion, sprang up, ready to cut the break short and jump into the pursuit. Don's experience spoke up first. It was important that no musher ever let another drive his team. The leader's dogs had likely just enjoyed a thirty-minute rest. For Don and Stan to short-change their teams in an attempt to keep up would only do more harm than good. It was wise and accurate advice, considering conditions. Unfortunately, conditions were soon to change. This was when absolutely everything went to hell.

It was darkness and wind, then deeper darkness and stronger wind. Another painful game of "Find the Trail" commenced with one extra twist. Stan's headlamp was fitted with the wrong bulb, and had been uselessly weak since the start of the race. Now Don's was dying as well. They were on the way to driving blind.

Amidst the blow and cold, Don rooted through his pack and found an old battery that he had previously discarded as dead. Now, he gave it a second chance. Running on a battery that was by all other standards depleted, Don's headlamp was still brighter than Stan's, which was running at full power. They had one light source back from the grave, and another on its deathbed.

As they crested a high mountain pass, they could see the leaders' headlamps in the valley below. All of them had fanned out, lost in the same storm. Stan and Don watched as the more efficient search party of eight repeatedly found then lost the trail. The advantage of being a part of a large pack was clear. With an array of high-powered headlamps, once the trail was lost, they could spread out and find it again in very little time. This gave them the momentum of a locomotive. Soon, those scanning beams grew distant, and disappeared from sight.

Without further describing the struggles of traveling at night in a snowstorm, this length of the race can be summed up with one fact. Traveling the first forty miles to Nome took the men sixteen hours, during which not a wink of sleep or comfort was had.

There was something different, though; something that set this storm apart from the winds of Shaktoolik. Don had made a change to the duo's typical leap-frogging maneuver. He drove his dogs as hard as he could, maintaining the lead through all of the worst terrain. For some reason, he seemed intent on taking the bullet, and giving Stan an easier ride. The result: Don's team was worn almost below the point of a slow trot. He had taken it upon himself to sacrifice his team's power on behalf of his younger teammate.

The sun came up after that long, sleepless night, and slowly, the wind went to bed. A few miles later, Stan and Don saw something new. A helicopter had touched down on the endless white tundra. Next to it, there sat seven columns of black dots; the leading dog teams. Stan and Don made their approach, and in a flash the seven leaders mounted their teams and sailed off into the snow.

The helicopter rotors were spinning up. It was a news crew, following leaders all the way to the finish. Stan and Don managed to grab the cameraman before he stepped into the bird. The cameraman told them what he knew. Among the facts was a devastating one. The leaders had just taken a two-hour rest in the snow. At this point in the race, that amount of rest was the equivalent to a brand new set of wings. Stan and Don watched as the helicopter kicked up powder, tilted forward, and resumed its course along the end of the Iditarod trail.

Silence fell upon them.

Stan's energy reserves, wherever he had been hiding them, kicked in. He bolted to his sled and got ready to make a run for it. He couldn't understand why Don was moving so slow at a time like this, but before he could give his teammate a pep talk, Don held up a calming hand.

"Stan, that's Susan and Rick up there. They have two hours of rest on us." It sounded like Don was gearing up for a "game over," speech, but that wasn't quite it. "There's no one behind us for thirty miles, we're in the top ten, and you're Rookie of the Year." He gave a warm grin.

Stan thought it over for a moment.

"We made it, friend," said Don. "How about we enjoy the last day?"

Regardless of how cold, taxing, and often miserable the past two weeks had been, a feeling surfaced that Stan didn't know he had in him. In another thirty miles, it would all be over, and he didn't want it to be.

Don gave Stan a pat on the back and a hit of coffee to keep him alive until they reached the finish line. They mushed off, taking in the scenery and quietly praising their dogs. During their brief layover at Safety, rather than a mad dash for Nome, the two sat inside the local roadhouse and enjoyed a bowl of caribou soup.

Barely awake, yet feeling very alive, they continued their way down the trail. Stan had no problem keeping up with Don, which made him think. If not for this man's good sportsmanship, Stan would undoubtedly have been at least thirty miles back, with the rest of the race. They had split the burden of storm-riding evenly between them right up until the final obstacle. After White Mountain, Don had taken it upon himself to push most of the way through the night.

There was absolutely no way that Stan wanted to pass a veteran that had sacrificed the strength of his dogs to help a rookie musher that was using a bum headlamp. If he wanted to, Don could have left Stan behind at any point in that night.

Either way, Stan would be in the top ten, and Rookie of the Year. Moving up from ninth to eighth place meant very little to him in the face of stealing a victory from his many-mile-mentor. So each time Don crested a hill and went out of sight, Stan called "whoa," and brought his dogs to a stop. It was tough to fool Don, of course, and one day later, after the race concluded, he would offer Stan a sincere thank you for holding back his team.

On March 20th, 1982, the young greaser who had walked away from a stolen car full of Christmas presents fifteen years before, passed beneath the burled arch at Nome with a time of sixteen days, six hours, forty-four minutes and zero seconds. He took ninth place, Rookie of the Year, and was awarded a check for $3,200. It was the most money he had ever held at one time.

The dogs received praise, food and rest. Chumper was given all of the above, plus fame. He was not yet two years old. The following days were ones of surreal calm. Stan was given a ranch house and truck, which belonged to a Nome local that was out of town. He visited the bars, spent time with the other mushers, and reminisced with Don. There was a level of mutual respect forged between the two men that would last the rest of their lives.

Stan rediscovered his love for interior heating and plumbing. It was as if every breath he took was another sigh of exhaustion and relief. He saw himself in the mirror for the first time in nearly a month, and caught a glimpse of the red windburn that bordered his eyes. Despite the incredible warmth and rest of those days, Stan found himself missing all of the people that had lifted him up and into the race. The storms, keeping up with their old ways, had prevented planes from flying in. Though the place still seemed to be bustling by Stan's standards, it was apparently only a fraction of the crowd that had formed at the conclusion of previous races. He had envisioned meeting Charlotte and Monica right at the finish line, but had been denied seeing them even the next day.

Stan had home on his mind. He had stories to tell and people to thank. Two days after completing the race, Stan boarded a Cessna Grand Caravan along with his entire team and sled, and was flown directly to Tanana.

From three-thousand feet over the air strip, Stan could tell that someone had been following his progress. He saw two fire trucks, the town cop car, and a procession of pickup trucks and four wheelers lined up next to the runway. As the plane's wheels touched down, the emergency vehicles blared their horns and flashed their lights. The Cessna taxied, came to a halt, and was immediately rushed by the people that had gathered to welcome Stan home. Charlotte and Monica were first to reach Stan. Then came John Hewitt, and Mike McCann, who, in his typical distaste for gratitude, explained that Stan had done one hundred percent of the work.

The dogs were loaded into a pickup truck so *they* could experience being driven somewhere for a change. Stan looked past the barking commotion to see Bill and Tom, who had rocketed him down the few remaining trickles of the Tozi River to the hospital after his bear bite. He saw Russ and Anne with their little toddler, Iris. Amidst a torrent of thoughts, Stan's mind flashed to the image of Russ, peering over his glasses at Stan that first Thanksgiving, when food was but a myth.

He was placed on top of the lead fire truck, just as its PA system blared a formal welcome to the 1982 Iditarod's Rookie of the Year. Behind the fire truck, Stan saw Jack and Karen piling into a car with young Robin, joining the parade. Both of their expressions were the perfect opposite of what Stan had seen the day he limped up to their house, years prior.

The ensuing parade was as fun as it was ridiculous. The PA chatter shifted from a hero's welcome to banter and wisecracking about Stanley, and his refined taste for dog food. Sirens and lights, normally reserved for emergency, were now setting every dog in every yard barking. The audience for the parade was minimal, though, as most of the town was participating in it.

Ringo and Joe were there, too, somewhere in the middle of the procession. Stan wondered exactly where he would have been at this moment, if not for their miraculous boatload of food, delivered ten long years ago.

He saw Joe Runyon, the man responsible for sending Stan on his first dog mushing experience, with a team of three dogs. It was a number that had grown over the years, though the count started with Joe.

And yet so many were absent. The older boy that had protected him, calling him "Stumples" all along, the people of Manson Creek that had welcomed him into what was truly a proving ground, the hitchhiker that had directed them to the plane, and the bush pilot that flew it.

Stan hadn't just traversed a one thousand mile race to meet this moment. He had gone from Boston to Manson Creek, to Terminus Mountain, to the Tozitna River, to Nome and finally, to the top of this very bright, red truck.

Reporters interview Stan beneath The Burled Arch, shortly after his race concluded.

Just past the finish line, Stan re-convenes with Don Honea.

Back at the homestead. Ninth place, and Rookie of the Year trophies.

Chapter 23
Found

July, 1982.

From above, the flowing current seems to be missing something. The ice has long since melted, providing a view of the clear-as-glass Tozitna River waters. The salmon are nowhere to be seen. When they finally do arrive, the fish have returned in drastically smaller numbers. The flood of 1978 had disturbed the salmon spawning process. Stan has no idea how he will feed his dogs. Meanwhile, time—
Swims on.

Stan's down-river neighbors pull back their nets, hoping to send as many fish as possible upriver to the man who brought salmon to the Tozi. The numbers improve, but not enough. Stan thinks back to his first winter on the river. He fears another one just like it is approaching. He knows for certain there are not enough fish to keep his dogs through winter.

There are days when distant pops of a rifle echo through the valley. Stan tries but fails to think of something, anything else while he brings his Iditarod team from twelve to six. Chumper and Sweeper will go on barking and wagging for some time to come. Grizzly, however, is silent now. Stan vows to never live another day like this one, and time—
Runs on.

Stan cuts countless planks and boards, milling them out of spruce trees with his chainsaw. He works obsessively, Grizzly and the other dogs that he put down still on his mind. The pile of lumber is large enough for a second cabin, but it won't be another home that he's building. He piles the wood high in a perfect square, leveling it by placing sticks between layers, allowing the wood to breathe. Next, he covers the pile in Visqueen, and is reminded of his old accommodations behind the hippy commune. Finally, he installs a stove in the center of the pile. It will burn all winter. The lumber will need to be dry if it is to float.

Time burns on.

Winter is busier than ever. Stan makes repeated trips to and from Tanana, hauling what he needs to get his project off of the ground. First to travel are five broken outboard motors. He hopes to combine their parts into three functioning motors. Next comes fifteen gallons of epoxy. Then nails, then fuel. Lastly, time—

Hauls on.

It looks like the bones of a beached whale. Stan erects the frame of what will bring him, his family, and all that he owns, off of the Tozi River. The planks go on, and he bends them into place. He layers the wood with three coats of epoxy, meticulously examining every square inch of its hull, popping the small bubbles that form with each layer. A glossy, waterproof sheen now covers the craft. The boat is thirty-two feet long, and eight feet at its widest. Its low weight and wide base allow it to float on just two inches of water. Stan mounts a thirty-five horsepower motor, and a one-fifteen on the craft's transom. He takes the ark out for a test drive. The water is still too low for them to make their move, and time—

Rushes on.

It's a big litter this year, and now there are thirty dogs at the cabin. The pack is far too large to feed through another winter, leaving Stan and Charlotte with only one option. If the pups are to live, they have to make it to Tanana before the cold sets in.

It's time to make a break for it. The massive boat takes on endless weight but doesn't sink. They load on two dog sleds, clothing, food, snowshoes, traps, tools, guns, chainsaws, one-thousand fish, thirty dogs, and one five-year-old named Monica. The boat floats well, high and strong.

Jack Bloom takes the lead in his eighteen-foot riverboat. He checks for rocks, overhanging branches, and riffles. As he encounters the threats, he calls out to Stan, who drops his anchor. After enough shallow water, the two men learn that Stan's ark, despite its weight, is floating higher than Jack's riverboat; where one scrapes the bottom, the other only glides.

Finally they see the mouth of the river. As they float into the wide and deep waters, Stan lowers his one-fifteen outboard motor into the water. As the monster engine roars, the boat hauls its massive load upriver, against the current, with enough speed to make Stan's hair blow. They make it to Tanana and time—

Whistles by.

Charlotte can see another life now. She aspires to school, and the start of her own career. She and Stan talk at length. One of them isn't willing to let their life end on the Yukon River. The other is. They agree that Monica would be better off with her mother, away from the frontier. As mother and daughter climb onto the small prop plane from the dusty airstrip, Stan is there to see them off. He and Charlotte are still friends, but no longer a couple. The Boston kid is a bachelor again, and time—

Drifts on.

He can't believe this twist of fate. Though he doesn't wear a uniform, he doesn't need to in a village this size. Stan has been sworn in as the one-man Tanana Police Department. He is often the first responder for medical emergencies, fights, and various crimes. He drives a cop car, not unlike the ones he had run from as a boy. In the summer, he prefers the fresh air, and rides freely around town by motorcycle. Though he still traps out at the Tozi cabin whenever he can, he's living in town full-time now.

Meanwhile, Russ Wood is entering the National Guard. Thirty miles upriver from town, his camp and fish wheel have just lost their owner. Not wanting the place to go to waste, he gifts the land and wheel to Stan. As he inherits the fishing operation, time—

Tumbles on.

He might be a little scared, but he's not showing it. Stan and a young, beautiful Athabascan woman named Kathleen are racing down mission hill in a freight sled, being pulled by eager dogs. Kathleen mixes her laughter with screams as the sled careens around bend after bend of the switchback trail. Stan compares the pulling power of his fourteen-dog team to his eight-cylinder hot rod. As the sled kicks up a cloud of fresh powder, time—

Races on.

Stan is in awe of Kathleen's wild spirit and her love of the woods.

They dance at the village hall, take long rides along the Yukon River, and talk of the lives they lived before. Kathleen grew up around fish at her family's camp, and could out-match Stan in a race to gut, fillet, and prepare a salmon. Stan tries to think of ways to get Kathleen to visit him more. Without much entertainment in his humble shack, Stan heads to the Tanana junkyard. Later, he presents his handiwork to Kathleen: two TVs stacked on top of each other. One plays audio, the other shows picture. Despite Stan's misguided strategy for impressing the woman, Kathleen visits more often, and time—

Flickers by.

Their son Joe is the ring-bearer. Their daughters Kate and Ariella are the flower girls. The ceremony concludes with a kiss, and so begins Stan's life with the native woman from the swift sled ride. Life settles down for the couple. In the summer time, they raise their kids at Russ Wood's old fish camp. It's a place of tall grass, white moths, barking dogs, and big salmon; all in the sloping sides of the Yukon River Valley. The kids learn how to handle fish, the fish wheel turns, and time—

Drifts by.

Stan's boat slides to a stop at the ever-expanding fish camp. His ponytail has turned grey now, but his Boston accent will never leave him. He calls up hill to Joe, who has already grown into his late teens. There's some exciting news that Stan can't wait to share. Someone, somewhere, is interested in putting him on TV. It's probably nothing. It sounds too ridiculous to be true, but—

Time will tell.

177

Thirty pups on the boat, ready to depart the Tozi, for Tanana.

Stan and Kathleen on the bank of the Yukon River, 1989.

178

Stan's home-crafted ark, still floating years after the move.

Inside the Tozi Cabin, as it looks today.

Epilogue

Tanana is a smaller, quieter place today. Both The Site and the hospital have been closed down, and vanished from the landscape, along with many of the people. Though the population is lower, its spirit remains the same. The village hall is sent into an uproar of dancing anytime the Tanana band plays, spring races are still held every year on the Yukon River ice, traditional hunting and trapping lives on, and the dogs still outnumber the human residents. Resting comfortably on the outskirts of town are Stan and Kathleen.

Every year as the river freezes and the snow falls, Stan gets into his parka, harnesses up his dogs, and whistles his way out of town to run his trapline. He splits his wood and hunts when he can. His little mechanical innovations have never stopped, from resuscitating old trucks, to fabricating a sausage maker out of a scuba tank and some piping. For short, very little has changed about Stan; even though it has been forty-three years since he landed on the Tozitna River.

Out there, in that old spruce grove, the cabin still stands. It couldn't be further from ruin, and the structure remains a well-preserved scene of those days in the seventies. Often in the winter, Stan travels out to the cabin to spend a night or two in the home that he made, and that also made him.

A great deal of Stan's time and energy now is devoted to sticking up for what is considered a main source of food for many people along the Yukon River. There is a definitive decrease in the size and population of the King Salmon run each year as a result of over-fishing. Stan's struggle to defend the Alaska lifeline is well documented in a great essay by Dan O'Neill entitled "Fall of The Yukon Kings," which I implore you to read.

On Tanana's Front Street, facing out towards the Yukon River, sits a low-roofed log cabin. There's a plywood sign, painted white with bold, black lettering that reads "TANANA TEEN CENTER." It is a substance-free place for the Tanana Youth to spend their weekends, created and operated by Stan Zuray. Inside, there is a pool table, board games, computers, and a TV with a few video games hooked up. When it opens every Saturday night, the cabin is filled with the scent of warm, fresh-made popcorn. As a requisite for the popcorn, there hangs an orange sign, stapled to the wall, its text is written in Stan's scrawl, which reads, "$100 Reward for the Arrest & Torture of Popcorn Spillers."

Every Saturday evening, Stan steps into the cabin, starts a warm fire, prepares the popcorn, and waits for the children to arrive. He hopes above all that, if they're lost in life, they won't have to travel as far as he did to be found.

Stan and Kathleen struggling to get the kids to stand still. From left:
Joe, Kate, and Ariella.

Stan's fish project, monitoring the Salmon run. Fish are scooped out of
the river, counted by camera and computer, and returned to the water.
Later years the system was upgraded, using microwaves to transmit
data and video back to a computer at camp ½ mile downriver.

The spot to be for kids in Tanana. Open every Saturday night of the winter, since 2010

Inside the teen center.

Stan enlisting the help of some Tanana children at his fish camp.

From top to bottom: Kathleen, Ariella, Kate, and Joe, 1991.

Out on the line, setting another trap.

Stan and Monica, today.

Stan's first selfie, taken in January, 2014, up on 14 mile hill, mid day sun low on the horizon.

Young Stan, bundled up for the Boston winter, heading out to get another car.

From Stan

Whenever someone told me that I should write a book about my life, my response was that I would be able to get it done once I stopped driving dogs, trapping, and fishing. In other words, never. It was sad, though. I always thought that it would be nice to see my life in print, just for my family and grandkids to have after I was gone. I think that's something that anyone would want.

I met Tim Attewell in Tanana years back, and he became a good friend of mine. He loved to talk about the life up here and was fascinated by the change that someone would have to undergo in leaving the big city to spend the rest of their life in the woods. When Tim asked if he could commit my story to words, I said yes for the same reason above: I wanted something for my family.

I always told Tim that this was his book; he was the writer. In return, he always said the book was mine; I had been writing it for sixty-five years. After working together for over two years, we've come to an agreement: it's our book, and I hope you enjoyed it.

This book never would have happened if my life hadn't gone the way it did, and I have a lot of people to thank for that.

My parents, Stan and Mary, raised me in a good home. They gave me love and a strong work ethic.

To my sister Mary and brothers, Andrew and Chuck , thank you for always being there for me.

My wife Kathleen and kids Monica, Ariella, Katlyn and Joseph – you are my reason to make it through each windstorm.

The people in Manson Creek accepted me into their community, and gave me my first real wilderness education.

The people of Tanana welcomed me into to their village. I'm proud to call this place my home.

There are many, very special hunters and fishermen of Tanana who have passed on. People like Freddy, Teddy, Lee, Percy, David, Roy and others are responsible for the skills I have today.

Lloyd Charlie of Minto was my first lifelong Alaska friend. He gave me my first sled dog and introduced me to "Indian Crackers".

The "River Rats" of Tanana took me under their wild and crazy wings when I first hit Tanana. Pat, Peter, Ken, Wayne, Tom, Laverne, Roy, James and Gary. Thanks for taking care of me.

Thank you Joe Runyon for the 3 dogs, harnesses, and sled to get me back to the Tozi after my first walk into Tanana.

Thanks to my neighbors on the Tozitna River, Jack and Karen, Tom, Bill and Kathy, Maria, and Russ and Ann. We were a great and caring community.

Lester Erhart has been my lifelong dog mushing mentor, never ceasing to amaze me with his ability to spot pups that will grow into strong sled dogs.

The late George Attla will forever remain my dog mushing hero. Thank you George, for being an inspiration.

Ringo McLaughlin and Joe Darbyshire saved me after the fire. I will never forget that day, or you.

Mike McCann not only gave me his friendship, but an incredible experience in The Iditarod that I will never forget.

I need to thank all of my sled dogs, past and present. You went through some incredible struggles with me, and took me places that most people could only dream of. My relationships with many of you were some of the closest I have had in my life.

Last but not least, I want to include everyone that Tim Attewell has thanked for helping him write this book. Many of you are my best friends. Thank you for making this book happen.

I now have that book that I've always wanted for my family, when I'm long gone.

Thank you Tim.

From Tim

I like to think that there's some kind of mystical force out there that pushes writers like myself into the lives of people like Stan Zuray. If such a power does exist, then I felt its influence when I was offered a chance to leave sunny Los Angeles and take a freelance television gig in Alaska. Having just been scolded for horribly botching a has-been pop star's coffee order, I was beyond enthused at the opportunity.

Stan and I met on March 19th, 2013. It was my first day in the village of Tanana, Alaska. Although it was 17 degrees Fahrenheit, everyone kept calling it a "warm day." When I stepped inside, out of the heat wave, there stood Stan and a few others. I had expected a firm handshake and a keen glare from a grizzled man waiting for me to prove myself as a true outdoorsman. Had that been the man I met, this book would not exist.

He was a man of short stature and easygoing nature with a thick Boston accent. I have pages of misspellings in my notes because of his unique pronunciations. "Don," was called "Dawn," his lead dog "Chumper," was written as "Chomper."

I knew Stan had left a potentially criminal life in Boston to be dropped off in the Alaskan wilderness, and I knew he had been attacked by a grizzly bear at some point. Most of what I gleaned was from mutual friends and fellow crewmembers; Stan himself boasted not one story. The man was humble.

As time went on, I gained the privilege of spending more time out in the bush with Stan. On the trail he was always quickest to offer food, or coffee from his thermos. At night he would leave the comfort of his sleeping bag every couple of hours to throw another log on the fire so we could all have warmth in the morning.

One night, sitting at a table with Stan and two friends near the end of my time in Tanana, Stan said that he would be willing to help put his life on paper. The next day, I said my goodbyes and parted company with Stan, as well as the village that had become the home of my life's greatest extremes.

So ended one job, and an entirely different one began. Endless, recorded phone calls were the story's lifeline. Sometimes I would reach Stan in his home. Other times he would get in touch through a broken satellite uplink from his salmon gathering home-away-from-home, called fish camp.

Stan gave me digital transfers from old VHS tapes of interviews he had done long ago. With this gold mine I was able to cross check Stan's facts. Both versions of Stan, old and young, corroborated one another's stories. As I quizzed Stan on the phone, he would give me the same mileage, numbers, and dates.

So the first person I must thank is Stan. His aversion to exaggeration, easy-going nature, and trust in my work made writing this book an absolute joy. I must move on, though, because there are many others to thank.

Residents of Tanana: You have been an inspiration to my work. Your village will always remain one of my favorite places on earth. Though this story consistently refers to your generosity, which allowed Stan to live the life that he did, not all Tanana residents are given the time and recognition that they deserve in this story. I hope you can forgive me if I have glanced over your contributions to this particular homesteader's life.

Every evening, around six o'clock, my lovely girlfriend Angel Bellmer asked me how writing went that day. Her support and the motivation she gave me are responsible for the book being released before the year 2020.

Brian Garrity and Al LaGarde hired me for my initial work in Tanana, and were very supportive of my writing once I returned home. I also have to pay homage and thanks to the co-workers that I lived with over the course of my time in Alaska. They are: Casey "Coos Coos" Goldberg, Chris Voos, Dan "Egg Boy" Eggiman, Eric Babisch, John Reily, Juan Fernandez, Kyle "Bedelly" Bedell, Mitch Buss, Ryan "Ry Guy" Walsh, Ryan Cahill, Scott "Scotch" Messier, Sean "B. Gone" Nichols, and Tim "Symmetry" Huten. Thank you Pat Moore for assigning all of those nicknames.

Mitch and Ryan were most directly responsible for my move, and

192

subsequent returns to Alaska. They also read an early draft of this story and offered mounds of encouragement.

Chris Pluchar, Mike Burke, and Becky Ullett took the time to read Stan's story, and helped me find the right questions to ask. The story is told in greater detail, and is probably far less confusing as a result of their feedback.

Kyle Douglas made it possible for us to publish this book, and did it with a smile.

Mike McCann is an inspiring Alaskan writer that listened to my whine when I thought getting all of this on paper was impossible. If you enjoyed reading this, you should definitely seek out Mike's book: "Give Me the Hudson or the Yukon."

Wendy edited the manuscript like a surgeon-poet. Reading this book would be a rocky road if not for her keen eyes.

Finally, thank *you* for reading. I hope you will make Stan's mantra your own, as I have:

"Perseverance Furthers."

Also By Tim Attewell

This story is a departure from Attewell's other writings, which are primarily science fiction.

"Marathon: An Introvert's Mystery Novella" Socially awkward Carl Pace must untangle a web of international espionage when a drug trial in his own body goes horribly wrong.

"Volt" In a world populated with living kitchen appliances and electronics, Archie Luthor smells a cover up when his ex-girlfriend is murdered.

"The Phoenix Seven" A short story about the events surrounding a mysterious bubble in time.

"Drag" A dark horror short.

Entering Stan into the Iditarod was only one of Mike McCann's many adventures. You can read about the rest in his book "Give Me the Hudson or the Yukon," which is available in paperback on Amazon.com

Printed in Great Britain
by Amazon